# ALL *Ladies* SHOULD USE THE F-WORD

## A GUIDE TO LOVING YOUR FINANCES

### KATHY COOK NOBLE

"*All Ladies Should Use the F-Word* is a must-read book for any and every woman who wants to fully understand her financial situation – both personal and business. Kathy shares real life experiences that will help you love your finances so your finances will love you back."

— *Bruce Cruickshank, President,*
*Top-Line Per4mance Ltd.*

"I have learned how helpful it can be to understand finance at an early age. It is especially important to ensure your independence and ability to care for yourself and your family. In *All Ladies Should Use the F-Word*, Kathy Cook Noble provides us with easy-to-follow and practical suggestions that to ensure our financial stability and future.

— *Lucy Jakupi- Haugen, Head of Learning*
*and Development for the Nordics and the Baltics*

"Although I am approaching 80 years of age I want to ensure my daughter and two sons will share equally in the assets accumulated during our lives. This book makes me realize that *now* I must learn and take action to guarantee this will happen without the government taking what our children and grandchildren have helped to amass. It is evident the information in *All Ladies Should Use the F-Word* is needed, both for myself and Canadian women everywhere."

— *Luella Monteith,*
*Retired Teacher*

"Kathy Noble has taken me from fear of finances to...someone who takes an interest. I may not be at "fun" yet but I learned that I do not have to know everything, and that there are tools and resources at my fingertips. With the information in this book, I recognized the need to look at my past relationship with money, my present situation and build a plan for the future. I am in awe of the stories and the successes Kathy's clients have experienced. These stories helped me find a path on my journey that is not only interesting, but hopeful.

Thank you, Kathy for the tough insight and hopeful, interesting path to financial freedom."

*— Sarah Hilton, World Class Speaking Coach,*
*CEO Spoken Advantage*

"I am so excited about this book for women. It continues to shock me how many professionals still do not have a handle on their finances and rely on the men in their lives to manage this. Having been through a dramatic shift in my life in my thirties and being forced to become aware, I am passionate about wanting women to be empowered, connected and aware of their finances. This book takes "the F-Word" from confusing and hard to manage, to simple and strategic steps to financial freedom. Kathy provides deep insights into the challenges we face, and shares practical solutions you can benefit from immediately. This is truly a must read for all women!"

*— Laurie Hawkins, Business Success Strategist,*
*CEO Hawk Inspired*

"A must-read for any woman who has always been intimidated by or struggled with finances. Kathy shares stories and personal experience that will help you learn to love your finances!"

*— Heather Puppa, Texas, USA,*
*Financially-Secure Investor*

"Through her eyes and honesty she guides her reader, on her journey of self discovery she brilliantly navigates us through her crisis' and how she successfully emerged on top. Kathy's insights have helped me navigate through my own personal crisis and financial loss, to someone who is starting to build a healthy relationship with my own finances. I totally recommend this book for anyone who is afraid of starting over or has lost a small fortune. Kathy's wisdom and passion to help others is evident in each passage. If you fear the F-Word then this is the book for you! Honest and straight forward Kathy's insights will help surely empower you to not only love your finances but to understand them as well. Once you understand finances you can succeed in life!"

*— Katina Kritikos,*
*owner Ethos Rejuvenation Centre*

"If you don't know Kathy and her work, you should. Kathy's sound financial brilliance gives her clients unabashed confidence about their futures. Her advice, stories and directions give women strategic steps to financial freedom -the F-Word is a manual for life."

*— Alyssa Light, On-the-spot Marketing Speaker,*
*The Profitable Innovator*

"This is the book I will be sharing with my book club; it is a must read for any woman who has been intimidated by or struggled with finances. Kathy shares stories and personal experiences that will help you learn to love your finances and give you peace of mind over your own financial security."

*— Fiona Roberts,*
*Municipality of Central Elgin Councilor*

"So much more than a finance book - this feels like a chat with a good friend - talking about life, lessons learned, and the bright future ahead."

*— Melanie Taylor, Facilitator and Coach,*
*The Achievement Centre*

"In my work with shifting people's relationship with money, time and time again, I bump up against perspectives that believe that "it's so complicated", "it's far to complex for me to understand", "Too many numbers, too little time", and the genius of Kathy Noble is, she makes it all simple... Make Money. Simple. That's it.... what if it could actually be that simple?? If you want to "Make Money.... Simple", read this book!

This book takes "the F-Word" from confusing and hard to manage, to simple and strategic steps to financial freedom. Kathy provides deep insight into the challenges we face, and shares practical solutions you can benefit from immediately. Yes! we are using Freedom and Finances in the same sentence!! Kathy can show you how.

I know a LOT about changing one's relationship with their finances.... but, WOW, Kathy's knowledge helped me understand so much of the nitty gritty practical stuff that I can apply right away. I feel excited about my financial future!."

— *Betty Mae Glen,*
*Wealth Health Expert*


"A must-read for any woman who has always been intimidated by or struggled with finances. Kathy shares her own personal struggle with family and business, how she moved forward beyond the drama and why now she is determined to change the story with women in finance!"

— *Christine McIver, Founder and CEO*
*of Inspired Choices Network*

Copyright © 2018 Noble Financial Solutions Inc.

All rights reserved. The scanning, uploading, and electronic sharing of any part of this book without the permission of the publisher is unlawful piracy and theft of the author's intellectual property. Please purchase only authorized editions, and do not participate in or encourage electronic piracy of copyrighted materials. If you would like to use material from this book (other than for review purposes), prior written permission must be obtained by contacting the author at kathy@noblecanada.ca.

Thank you for your support of this author's rights.

This book is presented solely for educational and entertainment purposes. The author and publisher are not offering it as legal, accounting, health or other professional services advice. No income claims are made or inferred in this work. You are solely responsible for your results. While best efforts have been used in preparing this book, the author and publisher make no representations or warranties of any kind and assume no liabilities of any kind with respect to the accuracy or completeness of the contents and specifically disclaim any implied warranties of merchantability or fitness of use for a particular purpose. The contents of this book are personal opinions and observations, based on author's personal own experience, and should not be taken as anything more than that. Neither the author nor the publisher shall be held liable or responsible to any person or entity with respect to any loss or incidental or consequential damages caused, or alleged to have been caused, directly or indirectly, by the information or programs contained herein. The advice and strategies contained herein may not be suitable for your situation. No one should make any decision without first consulting his or her own professional and conducting his or her own research and due diligence. You should seek the services of a competent professional before beginning any program. You are responsible for complying with the laws where you live and where you conduct business. You are solely responsible for the consequences of your use of this material.

The views expressed are that of the author and do not necessarily reflect those of The Canada Life Assurance Company.

The views expressed in this publication are those of the author. Kathy Cook Noble is responsible for the content of this publiation. GP Wealth Management and GP Capital Insurance and its affiliates are not responsible for and cannot accept any liability for any information in this publication.

Editor: Karen Rowe, www.karenrowe.com

Cover Design: Shake Creative, ShakeTampa.com

Inside Layout: Ljiljana Pavkov

Printed in the United States

ISBN: 978-1-7751634-0-4 (international trade paper edition)

ISBN: 978-1-7751634-1-1 (ebook)

*To all who have struggled financially; who want to understand their finances or are looking for better financial strategies, this book is dedicated to you. You are capable of understanding and controlling your finances. Take control now!*

# Table of Contents

# ALL *Ladies* SHOULD USE THE F-WORD

# Acknowledgements

With the support of friends and family all things are possible.

To my husband, Todd, thank you for always believing in me and supporting me, especially when I doubted myself.

To my sister, Karen, I can't imagine having made it through the past few years without you. Thank you for always being there to cheer me on.

To, my children, Tori, Hailey, Spencer and Gabby, thank you for the inspiration and for your encouragement.

I love you all.

# Introduction

This is the story of two women, Anne and Jessica, and
the choices they made. It's the story of money and spending, of splurging versus saving, and ultimately of what's
really important when it comes to our lives. It's about
finances, otherwise known as the F-word, and what happens when we've never heard it, and certainly never say it.

Anne and Jessica graduated from their small prairie college at the same time. Anne eagerly launched herself into
the work world. She took an entry-level job at a marketing
firm in Toronto and rented a downtown condo with her
boyfriend.

Anne left college with over $10,000 in student loan debt.
Tired of eating ramen, as soon as she began working she
decided to treat herself. She wanted to go out for dinner,
so she did. Her boyfriend was a spendthrift, so Anne would
foot the bill. Credit was in ample supply, as Anne always
made her student loan payments on time. Her credit score
was high, she had four different credit cards, and she
loved to shop.

Anne was optimistic as she began her career. She spent money on clothing, justifying the expense by saying she needed to look good for work. She went out every week with her colleagues, often closing the bar and spending nearly $100 every time. She shared her rent payments with her boyfriend, but he was a struggling artist who let Anne pick up the phone and electric bills. Anne never complained. Anne also never kept track, and never knew when bills were due.

As a result, she missed payments regularly, which led to the electricity being turned off one cold morning. Anne's boyfriend angrily blamed her. Anne couldn't understand. She called the company, and the representative told her she had missed several payments and would need to put at least $100 on the account in order to have the electricity restored. Anne gave the company one credit card; insufficient funds. She tried another; insufficient funds. Then another. Then the last card. Also insufficient funds.

Anne and her boyfriend fought about whose parents to ask for help. The fight grew in intensity, to the point where her boyfriend pushed Anne across the room.

Shocked, Anne grabbed her coat and left. She found a few dollars in her pocket, and bought a coffee, which she drank while scrolling the want ads. She felt desperate to leave her boyfriend yet knew she would not be able to afford first and last months' rent on her own. Her accounts were dry until payday. She felt trapped.

Meanwhile, across the country, Jessica was beginning her new life in Vancouver. She drove herself out there in her small Honda and rented a room in a house she shared with three other young women. They shared all the costs, from phone to groceries, and took turns cooking. Jessica loved coupon clipping and always found the bargains; they ate like queens most nights, and for very little money. She began working at a non-profit.

Jessica went out once in a while, usually meeting her girlfriends for drinks. She worked hard at her job, always setting aside 10% of her wages, 5% of that going into an emergency fund, the way her mother had taught her. The rest was for a trip to Nicaragua, where she was looking forward to volunteering with an international development team.

Since her wages at the non-profit depended on whether funding was granted, Jessica didn't worry when her position was cut. Her emergency fund was big enough to carry her through two months, which was all it took for Jessica to find a new job. In that time, Jessica was also able to finish some knitting projects, a hobby of hers, which she then decided to sell at the local Christmas craft fair for some extra holiday money.

When Anne and Jessica were in college together they would joke about their futures; who would be the first married, who would be the first to have kids. Jessica always figured Anne would be a CEO in no time; Anne knew Jessica would make a difference in the world. What neither women knew—or ever discussed—was just what impact money and their choices related to it would truly have on their lives.

Anne was trapped. She was in debt, with very few palatable options. Jessica, meanwhile, understood the need to be frugal and to plan for her future, when it came to managing her money.

Do you see yourself in either of these women? Are you an Anne or a Jessica? Don't worry if you're an Anne—you're most definitely not alone. I would argue that if you are an Anne, you are in the majority. When it comes to our finances—the F word—who teaches us to plan? Is planning instinctive? (hint: it's not.) Where do we go to get the answers we need? In an economy based on debt, what does it take to get ourselves to a state of being pro-active, not reactive?

Stories of women like Anne and Jessica are the reason I do what I do. I work with women who have been playing ostrich with their finances for too long. All it takes is one notice in the mail—the mortgage is due or a decade's worth of unpaid taxes must be paid—to make them realize they finally have to deal with it. That's when they come to see me; they want their financial stuff handled. Solve the problem. Make it go away. This is the attitude of the women I work with on a daily basis. These are women who are finally ready to take charge of their finances. Helping them is natural for me; I love to fix things, I always have.

I think finance is fun. I know there are plenty of people who would disagree. *How do they not?* I used to think. *It's so exciting. Doesn't everybody just love this stuff?* As it turns out, that's not the case.

I always liked math. I loved learning math tricks when I was little. In my early adult years, I did all the financing for a division of my parents' company. I witnessed a lot of our customer base get themselves into a lot of trouble with their money, and not always by choice. Life just happens. They got sick, they got divorced, they had crazy spending habits when they were younger. Sometimes they just had a lot of fun and made poor choices, and the only solution seemed to be bankruptcy.

What bothered me the most was that it was predominantly women I'd see in trouble. I saw that they were in trouble because they had bad relationships, with their

18

partners and with money itself. I saw so many disempowered women, women with no idea where their money went, even if they were the ones earning it! It struck me that women have been left out of this conversation for too long, and I decided to do something about it.

This is why I wrote this book. All women need to know the real F-word: Finance. I know it seems complicated at the outset, I know we've been conditioned to believe finance is a man's world. I know it's daunting to look at a stock ticker and understand the math behind a profit margin, or even just the concept of compound interest. It's daunting, sure, but here's the big secret no one wants you to know: It's not complicated.

You can understand it and I'm here to help you understand it. In these pages you'll find the basics of the F-word: everything you need to know about budgeting, investing, and planning for retirement. Not only do I share why all of this is important, I'm setting you up with basic, actionable steps you can start taking today.

The time for taking control of your finances and planning for your future is now. Now is the time. Not next year. Not when you're laid off. Not when you're injured. Not when your parents die. Not when you get divorced. Now.

# Chapter 1

# Where's your money?

"As a woman you are better off in life
earning your own money. You couldn't
prevent your husband from leaving you
or taking another wife, but you could have
some of your dignity if you didn't have to
beg him for financial support."

AYAAN HIRSI ALI, INFIDEL

Money is complicated. Right? Actually, no. It's not.

A lot of people believe that they have to watch BNN, CNBC, or CNN Money to understand the world of finance. Then, when they try to watch shows on those networks, they get all stressed and think they can't understand it. What most of those shows are discussing, however, are metrics that only those guys talk about. You don't have to be a trader on Wall Street (in the United States of America) or Bay Street (in Canada) to get a handle on your money.

Watching TV doesn't make you smarter, that's for sure; and when it comes to your money, you won't get any lessons on managing your finances from TV. Further, most shows on television are designed to make you feel inadequate; you're not smart enough, you're not competent enough to learn about your finances. You can't do it, so you have to watch a show, or buy whatever program they're selling.

They instill just enough fear in you to keep you believing you can't understand it yourself and that you can't do anything yourself. Most of the men on these money shows are old white guys, so you think you need an old white guy to show you how to handle your money, even if you're a black woman in your thirties. The reality is you can understand finance just fine. Most people are not sitting at home wondering how they'll manage six homes and a yacht and a plane when they retire. That's not their goal. For the most part, people just want to live a comfortable life, maybe travel a little bit more, and even then, not necessarily by private jet to a private island.

They just want to have the same lifestyle and carry on and be happy, leave something for their kids, and buy nice Christmas presents for their grand-babies. Most people are not thinking they need to have billions of dollars. On CNN and Bloomberg, everyone that they talk about are multi-millionaires or billionaires. The programming is designed to make you feel a little bit bad about yourself, or less smart. Stop watching TV and start getting real with your own bank account.

Beginning to understand where you're getting your financial information from is a good place to start, but getting wise financially involves a closer look at how you make the choices you make. As women, we have a long history of not asking for what we want. We're afraid to ask, because it sounds either greedy or selfish. In my own life, I took it for granted that I was going to run my family company once my parents retired. I never asked for anything. I never followed it up. I didn't want to be seen as greedy or self-serving. My whole purpose was to look out for the business and look out for my family.

In the next chapter, I'll tell the story of how my inability to ask let me down greatly. For now, I want to explain what I'm seeing. I'm seeing women with families and in business treating what they do as extensions of themselves. No one wants to be seen as greedy. No woman, especially, wants to be perceived of as selfish. As a result, women put others first, even above our own feelings and needs. Then, if and when things don't go right, we're left trying to figure out what we're going to do for ourselves.

What if we could flip the story around? What if it wasn't greedy at all to look after yourself? What if we could define selfish as *self*-ish, a way of taking responsibility for yourself and your well-being? As counter-intuitive as it may feel, trust me: it makes sense. It's exactly like putting on your oxygen mask first during an airplane emergency. You can't help anyone until you've got your own oxygen mask on. We learn this on airplanes every time we fly, yet still, to so many women, it's anathema to even consider putting ourselves first.

At some point in your life, you simply must put yourself first. The choice becomes, do you want to put yourself first in a planned way, knowing what you need to do to manage the bumpy road of life ahead? Or would you rather wait until an emergency strikes and it becomes an imperative to put yourself first because suddenly you're on your own? It's inevitable that something will happen in your life to force that closer look at your finances, and in my opinion, the readier you are, the more resilient you'll be.

You're better off to do it now when you can do it your-self, rather than having somebody force you to do it. When we're forced to do things, often we have to make decisions quickly, and while influenced by emotions heightened by the stress of the moment. Sometimes you don't have time to get all the information you need, leaving you to make deci-sions without sufficient knowledge. You don't have time to get a second opinion or expert help. As a result, you may not make the best decision, but you have to decide on *some-thing* because you've run out of time.

Imagine planning your retirement calmly with your planner one sunny afternoon versus breaking out your retirement plan because you're in the middle of a divorce. If you make the decision in advance you are being proac-tive, and the likelihood of you making a better decision sky-rockets. This is a healthier, more stress-free approach to managing your financial life.

Like most of us, I had to learn this the hard way, only I had the added advantage of loving math and being good with numbers. Still, after twenty years in the same place, I was forced to look for a new job and completely change the course of my life. Not only that, I had to do it amid a swirl of emotions as my family blew apart. For many other women, it's usually a divorce or separation, or becoming a widow, that leads them to this place where all of a sudden they have to deal with their finances while living through the biggest upset of their entire life. When the whole tra-jectory of our lives is changing is not the best time to make practical decisions.

Sometimes I meet with women who aren't necessarily in crisis or in urgent need, but who simply have no idea where their money is because they've left all the finances to their husbands. I've worked with women who didn't even know what institution the money was in or where their investments were. They had no idea how to access those accounts—and no clue as to where to start.

One of the biggest arguments that couples have is about money: how to spend it, and why they're in debt. According to Statistics Canada, for every dollar you earn, you owe $1.71. Basically, this means that for every dollar a Canadian earns, they are spending $1.71 – whether it's travel, credit card, housing, or student debt. It's not much different In the United States. In fact, at the time of print, student debt just passed mortgage debt! This is simply going the wrong way. It's clear that debt is increasing, and with it, so is our stress level. Money has an effect on you beyond whether you have any in the account when you need to pay for something.

Stress affects our body and health to a significant degree. Even if you want to do something like lose weight, a high stress level will keep you gaining weight. When you eliminate or reduce stress in your life, you have a much better chance at good health and happy relationships. Given that money is such a significant source of stress for people, doesn't it make sense to get it handled?

Getting your money straight will help you to diminish stress, and also make the home a more peaceful place. Instead of having kids grow up witnessing their parents fighting about money, they can learn money skills and enjoy spending quality family time together. Planning allows you to take the stress out of many daily choices; for instance, planning your weekly menu and budget for groceries lets you buy what food you need for what meals, while meeting your budget. It doesn't have to come down to wondering whether you can pay the hydro bill or get groceries every week, which is a stressful way of living. Instead, with some attention and diligence, you can determine what you have to spend, and whose responsibility it is to pay the bills.

It doesn't have to be complicated. It doesn't have to be a massive overhaul of your entire life. It's a good start if you just check your bank account once daily, so that you always know what you have and what you don't. Perhaps you go on to create a budget. These things take minutes, not hours. The biggest hurdle is overcoming the belief that it's complicated. It's not. The financial industry has made it look complicated, but if you're reading this book, you are more than capable of understanding the principles involved.

I have met many women who don't want to get a handle on this, who want to keep their heads in the sand. Through the years, several of them have come through my doors lamenting that they didn't start learning this stuff when they were younger. Taking care of yourself starts with getting your finances handled. It's not complicated, it's not difficult, and it's not beyond your capabilities. It is, however, something to start doing—and start doing now.

There's much to be optimistic about, however, as women in the world today. While I do see many women burying their heads in the sand, I see a new wave of women entrepreneurs who are inspired to get this handled, and to leave a legacy. These women have their own businesses, usually starting out with part-time ventures before transitioning into full-time, or sometimes just keeping the part-time work as supplemental to their primary income. Ventures like these are often in the direct sales industry; having parties or gatherings to sell cookware or other products, for example.

I asked Ronnessa Brown, a successful seven-figure entrepreneur who got her start in direct sales, to speak on the subject. Ronne teaches people all over the world how to leverage the direct-sales industry and earn income from home. She has helped women create six-figure incomes, become debt free, and live life on their own terms. Her recent book, *From Mopping Floors to Making Million on Instagram: 5 Steps to Building an Online Brand*, directly addresses the issue of women creating second incomes and taking control of their wealth. I knew she would be the perfect person to talk to about trends within the direct sales industry.

▼ **Ronne Brown's Top 3 tips for being successful in direct sales, or "home parties", as they used to be known.**

1. **Find a product that you love and market it**. The product you sell has to be something you enjoy and use yourself. It is important that you believe in the product and the company, and that you can stand behind it.

2. **Build your community**. Right now, women everywhere are shopping in stores less and less. Most are shopping online. It used to be celebrities who influenced how we think and shop, and what we buy. But now, companies are targeting everyday women because they are more relatable, more transparent, and attract a broader audience. Because of this, it's important to make sure you are transparent and authentic online. It is also why building your community is extremely important. With that influence and by building your community, you can monetize that community.

3. **Do not lose your personal brand in the process.** People buy you, *then* they buy the product that you stand behind. People in the direct sales industry often begin to look like a mascot, rather than a personal brand who is endorsing something they love. This is when you lose your personality, or step away from your authenticity. While marketing a product, don't let the actual product or the company wash out who you are.

Ronne is proof positive that direct sales is a huge growing market, especially for women. She believes it is absolutely sustainable as a second income. This is just one of so many opportunities for women today. This increased interest in entrepreneurship and the acknowledgement that they aren't completely comfortable with financial topics is a forward step for many women. They are becoming empowered to learn and take control of all aspects of their lives. Women certainly have the ability to understand their finances and are more than capable of running a business or starting a new one. When women have a community of support, either through an association or with a trusted advisor, they are capable of accomplishing great tasks.

*Chapter 2:*

# Learning Hard Lessons

> *"Take a deep breath, dust yourself off, and
> start all over again."*
>
> – FRANK SINATRA

Growing up, I had what I thought was a normal childhood. I lived with my mother and father, sister and brother. We went on family vacations and did all the things that kids do. The big difference was that we had a family business and it required a lot of time, energy, and conversation from everyone in the family. It always seemed to be the main topic of conversation at Christmas and birthdays, and across the dinner table.

I loved it, though. I loved school, too. Even when I started working full-time, I continued studying. I completed a master's degree in Business Administration (MBA), specializing in Finance. Then I did a master's in Strategic Focus. Hungry for more, I went for a third master's, this one in Public Administration. I also completed a Certificate of Adjudication. To say I liked school is an understatement. Once I got to school, I never really left. I graduated 11 times from 5 different universities.

The summer of 1995, armed with my business degree, I started full-time in the family business. I was 23. My family ran a total of 12 businesses, including a mini-storage, laundromat, commercial and residential properties, a gas bar, repair shop, detail centre, used car dealership, and land development. At one time we had a print shop, cabs and couriers, and limousines. It was all an amazing experience, and I learned a lot.

Since my undergrad was in marketing and human resources management, I handled all the marketing and advertising, human resources, office administration and health and safety training. I also did all the land development and leasing. As the businesses grew, I took on bigger and better roles. I would work ten hours a day, no problem, often working from home on weekends. If I wasn't there, I was still thinking about work. I was always the first one to get called if an alarm went off or there was some emergency to deal with. Within two or three years, I was essentially running the whole show, doing all the work but not legally owning the business. That went on for twenty years. I stayed single and just worked all the time.

The family business wasn't always easy. As much as I loved it, I should have realized there would be challenges. I knew this after the second year I had been there full-time, when I was doing all the marketing. We ran a very successful ad, but one of the managers didn't like it. He went to my dad and told him as much. Later, at home, my dad took me off that campaign because of that one manager. I acquiesced, expressing to my dad that if I was not able to do my job with relative autonomy, maybe I shouldn't be there because it would limit my ability to be successful and help the business. That was the first time my dad told me that if I left, they'd have to sell the business.

I couldn't stand the idea of the business not being successful, or being sold off to somebody else, so I stayed. Family has always been important to me—it still is—and I could see the potential with this business. I wanted to help it grow and do well and be massively successful.

In 1998, we began succession planning. My father never really, officially retired, although he slowly started coming in fewer days per week. We had a strong, solid succession plan. The only thing we missed was the final part of the execution. I trusted my parents. Who else would you trust? I was always told the business was going to be mine.

We did everything right. We just didn't execute the final part. It was no secret that I was the one who wanted to run and grow the business. There was total acceptance and agreement from my brother and sister, who didn't really have the desire to do it themselves. Frankly, they were happy to let me do all the work. And I was happy to do it. I liked it. The whole family was in agreement.

It turned out not to be the case. I didn't realize it at first, but my parents were really all about my brother. He's the youngest. He's the only son. He's the last of the name. I didn't realize it was like that. My challenge has always been separating the personal from the business. In retrospect, my downfall was focusing too much on the business and not enough on the personal. I focused too much and gave too much weight to the numbers. I didn't even pay attention to the emotions.

To this day, however, I don't truly know what happened. Between my siblings and me, there was no confusion. They thought I would be the one running the business; I always believed my parents wanted me to run the business. I learned that this is what happens when we don't account for how people think or feel. Somewhere along the way, I totally lost track of how I went from being the chosen successor, to not.

I've since learned not to assume anything. Not to be afraid to have the conversation and ask the questions. Even if you think it's authentic, have the conversations. You have to look after yourself.

Although I can't explain precisely what happened, I will say there was likely a strong element of control at play. When I decided to expand my life by dating and ultimately marrying a man who was as hardworking and dedicated to family as I was, you would think that it would be seen as a good thing. Instead, it triggered fears and insecurities that caused my family to act and behave in ways that didn't make sense. Part of that was wanting to control the business all the time. I think the fact that the planning and the succession had been in place, that we had done all that, showed that they did want me to run it, but the fact that they didn't actually transfer the business over to me revealed that they were not ready to give up control.

My mother was always very controlling, but after my father experienced some health challenges, around 2010, she became even more like herself. I think control as an issue is common in family businesses, whether it's trying to control other family members or trying to control everything that happens, and the reality of a family business is that you can't control it. When people accept this and learn it early, then everybody's more successful, both business and family, and you're able to stay a family, stay friends, and stay successful. In our case, it was easy to take advantage of me because I loved the business, so I would accept a wage that was sub-par, and long hours, and doing all the work that people didn't like, because I loved it. I loved business.

As we expanded the business, my dad asked that I put a franchise that we purchased in my name, as it would make new business start-up loans available to us.

From the bank's perspective, they wanted somebody in their early 40s with my background. They were happy to have me as the person of record and expand with me, rather than work with someone in their early 70s. It made sense.

The building and everything else were in my parents' name. The only things I had in my name were the loans. From a business perspective, on their side, it was really a good strategy for them because they owned all the assets and I just owned the debt.

I kept my dad in the loop, showing him the plans, asking his advice as we picked out equipment for the franchise. I kept him involved in the process, and he was part of all our meetings with Head Office. I never gave it much thought because I was going to own the business someday—and I trusted my parents.

It wasn't until I found out that my parents had been talking with a lawyer behind my back that I began to pay closer attention. They had concerns about the franchise not being in their name. After all, what if I quit or wanted to leave the business?

My brother had the title of manager, despite the fact that he had no one to manage. He did clean-ups for car leasing and the department he managed was shut down to the public: we only ran it internally. Although he believed he worked really hard, his work was sporadic and inconsistent. Still, I covered for him for years. I did his work and never said a word. I also lived beside my brother for years, but I never reported on his lifestyle to my always-inquiring mother. When I finally did concede that his behavior was less than ideal, my mom instantly pounced on me for being mean to my brother. I was baffled.

The succession of the business was a non-issue until I got married in 2014. I married Todd, the man who had done all the construction and renovations for the franchise. He became the service manager, and we worked well together. We built the company through increased sales. The ownership was never a thought for me. However, my mom became obsessed with controlling the franchise, and soon she and my father were very concerned about the franchise not being in their name. My parents' tagline seemed to become, "It's mine. I own it." I heard it for a very long time, and I never argued with them. I knew the business would be mine someday. Still, my parents and their endless refrain of "It's mine. I own it," eventually wore me down, and I finally acquiesced. "If it's yours, then come run it," I said. "I'm not fighting for it."

I never fought with them for anything. And I signed everything over. After I had spent 20 years building the businesses up, I signed over the franchise for $1. Then I signed off any future shares. Then I walked out of the business with no future, no job, and a pile of debt from professional fees that I had to pay to have someone represent me to finalize the release from the business (to protect me from my parents) on what I never asked to have in my name to begin with. On top of that I had to sign a non-compete clause for all their industries. To add insult to injury my husband lost his job too. The amount of debt I left with was equal to a mortgage on a house but without a house.

The situation split my family in half, dividing us right down the middle. My sister and I were on one side and my parents and my brother on the other. My sister and I are very close and our parents and brother no longer speak to us.

My brother created drama and would complain to my parents when he didn't get his own way. I don't like drama, and I didn't participate. Of course, it was the only soundtrack surrounding me, so it was inevitable that I was affected by it, despite my efforts to stay neutral.

For years, I had taken care of everything in the business. I did strategic plans. I did all the reports. I was the one to hire and train the staff and to attend to all the legal matters. In short, I did all the hard work to implement their idea. I got taken for granted and, in the end, I got royally screwed.

Despite talking with several lawyers, all of whom confirmed I had a case, in the end, I just couldn't sue my parents. I was never a negative person, but during this time in my life I was shocked, upset, disappointed and angry. I didn't want to linger in this place, so I decided against a lawsuit. I still can't believe it happened.

The bank manager confirmed that having me on the hook for everything and running the business was good for the bank and the business. However, to remove me from the debt, we were making a poor decision for the company. He did, however transfer most of the debt over to the company itself, promising me they'd sign it over and get me out. My parents had to have everything. Although they were legally obligated to pay me, I never did receive a wage that year, nor was there any severance. But I didn't want to have to fight my parents for it.

It was bad, however. I had redone the mortgage on my house using a home equity line of credit because it was required to have equity in the franchise in order to secure the small business loan. I put $30,000 of my own money in to get the franchise, to show equity and to get the small business loan. I never got this money back, as my parents refused to give me anything.

I had also had a bank account since I was 15, a joint bank account with my mother. She never, ever withdrew money. Only once in a while, before there was direct deposit, would she put my cheque directly into the account, as the bank was on the way to her house. Other than that, she never went near it. It was my account. Of course, I'd forgotten it was a joint account, and two days before my mortgage was due, just before the holiday weekend in July, she went in and drained my account. It was nasty.

Nobody understood it. But it seemed a lot of people who knew our family weren't that surprised. They were surprised I didn't know how favoured my brother was or how I'd failed to notice that some family members were overly focused on the money. I had a hard time with that because I had never seen it that way. I know there was a lot of money involved and my grandpa made a lot of money, but I never thought of it as free money. I just wanted to work hard. I never really gave it the credit that I should have. My Grandfather had worked hard, as the first generation of the business, and enjoyed the business success while he was alive.

This story is heartbreaking to share when I write it, I still have a hard time believing that it truly happened... it seems like a fictional story. I can attest to the fact that it is real and I have only touched on the highlights that I believe can inspire change for others. I can tell you it is real because ...

it is my story. It was my experience with my family and our business. It taught me many lessons, many difficult lessons that have equipped me on my journey to guide others to be more aware and protect themselves from living through experiences like this.

The lessons this has taught me when it comes to succession planning have been profound. Here is the critical distinction between how they thought of succession planning and what I thought: Their idea of succession was, *"When I'm dead, somebody takes over the business."* That is the crappiest form of succession you can have because it doesn't give anybody any opportunity to ask questions or transition effectively. It's bad for staff. It's bad for banks. It's bad for investors, if you have them. I believe succession should be a smooth and seamless transition from one person to the next. They should work together on the plan, the timing and the announcement of when it will happen. I especially believe it's important for a company to be viewed as a going concern. This means that the insiders see there is a strategic plan and the outsiders see there is an on-going commitment to the business expressed in the transfer of leadership.

Knowing what I know now, I would have said let's get things executed. Follow up. Get it done. As much as you may want to be a trusting person, you have to do it professionally and in writing. I'd also value myself instead of putting myself second to everyone else. As often was the case, I'd do everything for everyone else before I looked after myself. Business is separate. You can love your kids equally as family members, but in business they're not always equal and that's something you have to make sure you really understand. The business is its own personality. It has a culture and a direction and a purpose and people fit into it. You don't make it fit everybody else. If you want a business to succeed it's got to be respected and handled right, and that means you look at it objectively and determine the best way to handle your money. This applies to your own money as well, whether you come into an inheritance or just amass amounts of it through your working life.

If someone had come to me five or ten years ago and said, "Kathy, you have to execute your succession plan," I wouldn't have listened. I would have said, "I trust my dad. I trust my parents." Here is what I say to that now: "You can trust your parents all you want. But as people age, they may go through challenges that make them fearful of change. You also have to make a good move and you have to show your staff and, your investors, your bank manager, and a lot of other people strength and continuity in the transition, because it's not just you who has a stake in that business. When you are in business and have employees, their families and their future are affected by the success or failure of the business. The ripple effect is real and important.

If your staff and your siblings lose their jobs, they can't pay their mortgages or buy groceries. You have to respect everybody else involved to say you need to execute the transition because you need to show the world that this business is a going concern and that the torch has been passed and it's going to pass again.

I had even done estate planning for myself. I had a life insurance policy, for the future, that was going to cover the taxes and the growth for when it was my turn to pass the torch. People have to see that the business is going to carry on, that it's going to stay a strong pillar in the community and that their job is safe.

A lot of staff left when I did, even though I tried to reassure them it would be all right for them. I encouraged them to stay. Some stayed for a few weeks, some a bit longer; but ultimately a lot of great staff were lost. It had taken a long time and effort to build a great staff and work environment, and both were quickly undercut.

If I hadn't had savings I wouldn't have survived this total life readjustment. I would have died, financially. There were some comments I had heard about my parents trying to bankrupt me. I was determined not to let that happen. I continued to work in the family business and not get paid for close to a year. I had to keep working. I had no sign-off on the business debt. I was still responsible for the loans. So, if I didn't come into work and anything happened, I was on the hook.

It wasn't a lesson I really felt like learning, but if I hadn't saved and built up an emergency fund, I would have been desperate. As it was, my partner and I had a shaky time navigating that year. How are we going to pay for our wedding? We had our wedding money, but ended up having to use that money just to pay for my house. We had two households that we needed to sustain until we were married.

More and more, however, support came out of the woodwork. I learned that my parents really were focused on my brother: he really was the favourite. I couldn't understand how everyone else knew this but me. It's a common occurrence to see the son in the family given more, whether in business or in the family in general. This was certainly the case in my family. My brother was placed on a higher tier than his sisters.

I always thought I was the favourite. I never had a problem with my parents. I never went through a phase when I was a teenager. I was never, ever a problem. I never got in trouble for anything and I thought I must be the favourite, right? And I didn't see that. Like, really? The son? That's so cliché.

I believe kids can be equal in the family, but they can't be equal in the business. I got caught up in the times and I assumed my family was with me. By the times, I mean, we live in an age where the son doesn't actually have to be the one to run the business. Women have been running businesses for decades. The idea that the business would go to the son just because he's a man strikes me as quite old school, frankly. What happened opened my eyes, however, and reminded me just how far we still have to go in terms of gender imbalance in the world of business. The irony, of course, is I worked in a predominately male industry and negotiated deals, managed staff, dealt with suppliers, etc. Almost all of these negotiations were males and I did this with no issues or problems.

Even if I had insisted on executing a succession plan, chances are my parents wouldn't have followed through. They may never have had any intention of executing the plan, I don't know. The only benefit to me is that I would have had more time to recover any lost expenses. I would have been in a better position to say, "This is not for me. I'm not prepared to make a crappy wage and not have a secure future."

It's tough, but you have to have the information. A lot of it sucks. It was a terrible thing and I never would have thought it would ever happen to me. Even when I went through this I kept thinking, wow, that poor girl, like I was having an out-of-body experience. I couldn't believe a family could do that to their daughter, a daughter who had given her all to the family business.

This is why it's so important to me to help women galvanize themselves against ever losing control of their finances. Nobody should have to go through that. Trust is great, but you really have to protect yourself. Trust with a little bit of protection is better. It was a good lesson. An expensive lesson, but a good one.

In the end, however, good things always come out of adversity. I am closer now than ever with my sister. I met and married my husband and we are now in business together. I get to run my own business. Now the stuff I used to do for fun – financing and bookkeeping – I get to do full-time.

If I could distill what I learned, I suppose it might look like this: first, get help. Solid help. Be willing to speak up, take a break, re-evaluate, and get a second opinion. Trust yourself. Respect yourself and stand up for yourself. This is hard for a lot of us, but it's essential. We also have to deal with things head-on. I know a lot of women are afraid to do this, and don't want relationships to fall apart over money. Still, we need money. We deserve to live and deserve to be well paid and valued for our work. Finally, understand that what may not be important to you is very important to others.

Most of these lessons are considered innate masculine ways of doing business. I had to learn them. Women do things differently, and business does not at all need to be synonymous with a masculine way of doing things.

Empowering women to take control of their finances is important to me. It builds confidence; it gives hope. Finances are one of the big blocks women put in their own way. They underestimate their ability. I want to empower women to be confident to make their own decisions.

# Chapter 3

# Run Your Own Life

*"If we were not impressed by job titles, suits, and jargon, we would demand that financial advisors show us their personal bank statements before they tell us what we could or should do with our own money."*

MOKOKOMA MOKHONOANA

The very first step towards financial freedom is simple, one you can take today: Know where your money is.

I realize this book contains predominately Canadian references; however, the concepts are still the same in the United States, and almost everywhere around the world. When I reference specific Canadian financial tools, keep in mind that differences between Canadian and American investing exist, and this is why seeking out an advisor you are comfortable with is important to help with your financial plan.

Let me tell you about my client, Mary. She is 52 years old and almost my perfect client. She had a lot of money, and on the day of her first appointment, she came to me straight from the bank. She told me that while the woman she had talked to was very, very nice, she never really explained anything. Mary had no idea what accounts her money was in. Her husband used to take care of all the finances and, now that they were divorced, Mary had no idea what the plan was, or if her money was making money.

Further, Mary had found out that her husband had never paid their taxes, and they were in debt. She was overwhelmed and desperate to understand. The bank advisor hadn't offered the information Mary sought; Mary didn't really know exactly what to ask to get that information.

People are usually skeptical of financial advisors to begin with. The industry is perceived to be full of people who are untrustworthy and out to steal your money. As a financial advisor myself, I always want to help people get organized before I start making suggestions. In Mary's case, I went through her statements and reviewed her investments with her. I showed her where her money was invested, and how it was doing. I learned that she was already tracking her spending, which is great. You don't always need a budget, *per se,* when you're always tracking what's coming in and what's going out. What's important is that you have a spending tracking system – and that you always have less going out than coming in.

I put together a plan for Mary, which sold her on my service. She hired me to look after her money, and we put the plan in place. When we were wrapping up, Mary looked at me and said, "I've never understood any of this until now." I reminded her that she needs to understand.

She doesn't necessarily need to know where to put her money in terms of investments, but she needs to know where her money is, how it's doing, and what the plan is with it. I like everyone I work with to feel comfortable knowing they have money in an emergency fund. Money for a trip they're taking that they're saving for. Money for home renovations. Money for retirement. I offer people a level of comfort. Knowing where their money is alleviates a significant amount of anxiety.

Around the world, women tend to live longer than men. This means that, at some point, most women are going to be forced to look after their own finances, whether they like it or not. And that could happen at any age, really. If you get married at 25 and you're married for 50 years and your partner passes, you're still left by yourself even if it's only for a relatively short time. It doesn't matter by how long you outlive your partner, you still have that time, and you'll have to be responsible for your finances during it. It's not *if* it's going to happen: it's *when* it's going to happen. Nothing lasts forever: the car needs repairs, the dishwasher might blow up, we lose our loved ones.

For women, once they become the one who has to look after their finances, either because of divorce or death or whatever the case is, you have to know your money stuff. If you have a broken arm, you go see a doctor; if you have a toothache, you see a dentist. If you want help with your money, go talk to a financial advisor.

Through my years in financial planning, I've observed three common concerns most women have. The first is that they don't think they have enough money to invest. People in general, but women especially, think that you have to have a lot of money to start investing, that it's something fancy or something only the wealthy can do. The reality is, you can start investing with as little as $10 a month. I have a client who was just starting out, trying to save money with a young family. We found an investment opportunity at $10 a month and she started there. I ran an illustration for her to see what that money could grow to. For example, with $10 a month, investing for approximately 40 years, it could grow to almost $45,000 with a conservative outlook. That's the power of compound interest. She can take a total of $5300 (total of the $10/month over approximately 40 years) and turn it into almost $45,000. The added excitement was that this was being done in a tax-free investment, so she would have all the money to use for herself.

Just start with what you have. Within a couple of months, you might double your investment to $20 per month. The whole point is to just start the habit. It's getting into the mindset of saving or investing. It's a discipline, sure; but once you've made the flip, it's not long before you put down that beautiful leather handbag because you know that by not purchasing it, you've just bought yourself a night in Cancun on vacation.

The second biggest concern women have is that they feel stupid asking questions. I actually blame the financial planning industry for that. I most certainly have come face to face with advisors, and even whole companies, that don't make people comfortable enough. These people deliberately try to make things sound more complicated than they are or give the impression that you have to be licensed or have a certain level of education to actually understand it. I'm here to tell you that, believe it or not, you too can understand your own money.

I have open and honest conversations with every client I see. I want to talk about where they're at and it's vital to me that they're comfortable understanding what's theirs. I ensure a space that's open for all questions—after all, there are no dumb questions—and invariably, as I answer their questions, I notice the relief start to creep in. At the end of a session, my clients leave feeling so much better, just because they were able to ask their questions.

The third biggest concern the women I work with have is that they're afraid of losing money. I think women are more risk-averse than men. I understand this, so I always have an open, honest conversation about what it is that we're looking at doing, what products we're looking at investing in, and then, within those products, what specific funds we're looking at investing in.

Before we even get to investing, however, I always start with an honest conversation. I begin by asking about my client's source of income, including how stable it is. I want to know how they are managing their daily expenses, mortgage, groceries, bills. I ask about debt load and get a picture of where they're at, listing all debts they may have, even interest-free loans from family. Then I check in around what they have in place to protect their income. If there's nothing in place like disability or critical illness insurance, I encourage them to get on board with the right kind of insurance for them. I also need to know what—if anything—is set aside for emergencies. We discuss an emergency fund.

The last thing we talk about is investing. Usually in the case of an emergency the first thing we do is cash in our investments, so I like to get a clear picture of the situation, get the debt under control, ensure they're on track to have a minimum of three months of living expenses in their emergency fund, and then we talk about investments.

The reality of investing is that the market goes up, and the market goes down, so we discuss how risk-averse the person might be. How much risk can you handle, both fiscally and emotionally? Over the long term, we want it to be doing better for your portfolio than not, and we do that by having annual meetings, open communication, and making sure that the products we pick and the investment tools we use are appropriate for each person. I'm a big fan of diversification, not just diversifying the fund you have or fund companies but the vehicles you use so that you don't put everything in the same investment.

Once they're comfortable with the information I've shared in our discussion, I do the paperwork and submit it to the various fund companies. I create custom plans for all my clients and keep everyone updated regularly. I make sure I'm available to receive calls or set up meetings any time there are issues. I keep the conversation open, so we keep exploring my client's financial options. We manage the money together, and there are no secrets.

That's a glimpse into how I work. Is this common among advisors? I certainly hope so. Keep in mind, if you're looking for an advisor, that you should shop around. If you feel you don't even know enough to compare services, feel free to ask advisors if you can contact a former or previous client. Most advisors can give you the name of at least one person to call as a reference.

Advisors are paid one of two ways; they're either paid by the company they have you invested with, or they are paid directly by you (this is known as a fee-based advisor). Simply put, working with a fee-based advisor means sitting down together at the table and asking the advisor to do your plan for you, then paying them directly. Working with a commission-based advisor means the company they invest with pays the advisor's company a commission, and they are paid based on whatever their contract is with that company.

When it comes to deciding the best approach, consider your investment returns. Are you making money? If you're making 10 or 12%, does it matter if your advisor collects 2%? Or what if you're making 3% on your money, does it make sense to pay a fee then? Just like in any industry, you have to look at the exchange; does their service match what you are paying them in terms of value? You could pay someone $50 an hour and they might do a terrible job for you, or you could be paying someone $100 an hour and they may be saving you lots of money or making you lots of money. If you get your car fixed, you might pay a lot for the right mechanic but what you're paying for is not just their professionalism and expertise, but also knowing that your brakes won't go out on you as you drive. The alternative is thinking you've saved money by choosing the cheaper mechanic, but having your brakes go because that mechanic wasn't as good. It's the same with choosing an advisor.

Advisors work for you. It's your money, and you're making the decision to work with them and have a relationship. You make the decision. They have the expertise, but you're paying them, they work for you. It's their job to do what's right for you. If you don't have good feelings about it, it's easy to move on.

Trust your gut. If you like the person and feel comfortable with them, comfortable enough to ask questions, then you're probably on the right track. After all, you're not buying the product, you're buying the person. I know you think you're buying financial products, but you're really starting a relationship. You will be working with this person who will know your finances and other intimate details of your life and you might be in this relationship for decades. You've got to be comfortable calling them up at any time and asking questions without feeling like you're bothering them. You never want to feel bad asking a favour of someone you're paying to advise you.

If you are still unsure about someone, you can also check regulatory sites to ensure they're actually licensed and have no charges or issues pending. This does not seem to be as big of a deal in Canada; however if you're reading this in the US it's always a good idea to do a regulatory background check.

There are also pros and cons of working with a big company versus a smaller shop like mine. When it comes to the larger companies, it's important to check whether the advisors have to meet quotas. If they do, you risk getting steered into something not necessarily right for you. Other companies might be very big but their focus is on high net worth, so if you don't meet the threshold of a certain dollar amount, you might not get the same quality service (even though you still deserve it) that a high net-worth client will receive, because you're just not part of their mandate. It's just how they're steered.

The advantages of going with a bigger company are these: they've usually been in business for a long time, have experience, and have access to more products. Then again, some of their products may be proprietary, and large institutions sometimes only offer their own products. If the

50

product is good, then great! But if not, well, you're getting it anyway. In my case, although I'm associated with a big Managing General Agency (MGA), I have flexibility and no allegiance. This means that, while I have access to all the companies, I'm not obligated to any particular one. This way, I can do a comparative analysis between companies and get the best program for my client, and I'm not under any quotas or obligations to do that.

The other advantage to the way I do things is that I still have access to a bigger company. In my case, I have access to an estate planning department and I can get help in that area. If I don't have expertise I can find someone who does. You can't be the expert on everything.

I've also had people ask me if I'd be willing to work with another advisor. I don't see this as a problem; why not be cooperative? I know, however, that many advisors are against this and want to work alone. The risk to having multiple advisors is that balls might be dropped; you might find your kids' education fund is on track while no one has looked at your retirement planning. The advantage to having multiple advisors, however, is that you always have a second opinion: more information or viewpoints with which to make your decisions. The best solution is either to work with one advisor, or, if you do go with two, ensure they're working together and you're covered. It's up to you and your comfort level.

When you work with an advisor you should meet with them a minimum of once every year, unless something life-changing happens, like you have a baby or lose your job or something like that. This way, it makes it easy to add in things that you need, take out stuff that you no longer need, or make adjustments to your portfolio. It's also not stressful; consider it maintenance, really. Once a plan is set up, it's easy to maintain.

Before you get an advisor, however, I've created a handy to-do checklist to help you understand what needs to happen when. The financial to-do list is a guide to help you get started. It doesn't have to be done in exactly the same order that we have it listed, but it helps to have a starting point. One of the biggest hurdles to overcome is that feeling of being overwhelmed, of not grasping something quickly enough. I hear all the time, "I don't have time. I don't understand. I'm not smart enough. I don't have enough money."

If you've heard those phrases come out of your mouth when talking about finances, this checklist will help you. This is a way of seeing it's not about whether you have enough money, or whether you have an MBA. It's not about having a financial advisor or not having a financial advisor. I certainly believe they help if you have the right one, but if you have the wrong one, it could get you into trouble. The financial to-do list is a starting point. For example, you don't have to have a budget in place and be following it and have that under control before you prepare a will, but you should have a will. Having a will is the easiest and best place to start because it takes care of your children. There are many ways that you can get a will done, which we will discuss in chapter 7.

This financial to-do list is a way to get the conversation started. It's also something for you to look at. It's tangible. You can see it in front of you, so you don't have to remember all the details. It also helps you guide your financial future for the kids.

If you have a husband or a partner, a close family member or a friend that's going to be part of the process with you, either as your executor in your will or as a guardian to your children, it also helps them to put into perspective what your situation is.

If something happens to you, it's easy for them to be able to look through and say, "Okay, I should be looking for certain things. I should be looking for a bank account. I should be looking for a life insurance policy. I should be looking for an RESP (Registered Education Savings Plan) for the kids or a TFSA (Tax Free Savings Account)."

Once you have the to-do list in place, it keeps the momentum going. It makes it easier to master your finances, and it makes it fun. You get to check stuff off the list. That can lead you into doing some really great tax and estate planning with your advisor, so it all flows nicely together and helps to make you and your family successful.

Below is a chart I use to show my To-Do list. Feel free to print it out or download a pdf version from **www.WomenWise.ca**. In the following chapters, I'll go through each step and explain why that item is useful, and what you can do to start implementing it in your life immediately.

# Financial To-Do List

| PRIORITY | DUE DATE | WHAT | WHO | IN PROGRESS | DONE |
|---|---|---|---|---|---|
|  |  | Budget<br>Set a household budget, review regularly and amend as needed |  |  |  |
|  |  | Prepare a Will<br>* If done by and held with lawyer then make sure someone knows who your lawyer is.<br>* If you do it yourself, make sure someone knows where it is. |  |  |  |
|  |  | Bank Accounts<br>- Make sure daily bank account is not charging a lot of fees (or none at all).<br>- Set up on-line account for savings, example Tangerine. |  |  |  |
|  |  | RRSP<br>- Get retirement plan set up and contributions made, if appropriate to your financial situation. |  |  |  |
|  |  | TFSA<br>- Set up a Tax Free Savings Account and make a contribution, Use in emergencies, or as retirement savings, if appropriate to your financial situation. |  |  |  |
|  |  | Children:<br>RESP- Set up education savings, if you are planning on your children attending post-secondary education, if appropriate to your financial situation. |  |  |  |
|  |  | Life Insurance<br>-either get a pure life insurance policy or a hybrid life insurance policy with investment options, this depends on your financial goals and planning |  |  |  |
|  |  | Children's Life Insurance:<br>-set up hybrid life insurance policy with investment options as soon as possible if appropriate to your financial needs. It is can be very inexpensive, it pre-qualifies the children and sets them up for their future |  |  |  |

# Chapter 4

# The Benefit of the Budget

*"We are what we repeatedly do. Excellence,
then, is not an act but a habit."*

-ARISTOTLE

I'm sure you've heard the basic money advice: live your life within your means. What exactly does that mean? For me, this expression means the cash that comes into your house is greater than the cash that's going out of your house. You're buying what you need, you're enjoying your life, you live in a house you can afford, you drive a car you can afford, you go on trips you can afford. You're saving for your future, and for your retirement. You are able to enjoy going out with friends for coffee whenever you want to, or for dinner or to a concert. Living within your means allows you to enjoy your life the way you want to enjoy it without feeling the stress of money.

The reason people don't do this, in my opinion, is that there's so much influence on us from the outside world. The concept of "keeping up with the Joneses" persists, perhaps even worse now with social media. We look around and see our neighbours living better than we are, with more expensive cars or clothing. We have a need to compete with the people we see outside of our homes, rather than take a closer look inside of our homes to see if we're doing the best job we can for ourselves and our family.

We live in a world where many people place a lot of emphasis and importance on money, and there is almost constant conversation in the media on the topic. Images of celebrities with a lot of money bombard us everywhere we go. So much of this is flamboyance and quite unrealistic in some circumstances. My suggestion is to take the focus off of money and stop giving it so much power. It's just another thing you need during the day. You need air to breathe. You need money to buy food. It is what it is. It's just another piece of the puzzle in our lives, so don't give it so much power. Focus on addressing your needs, first and foremost; if you're in debt, focus on getting out of debt. Focus on saving for your future.

In modern society, and especially for us as internet users, images of all the things other people have or are doing surround us constantly. It's also all too easy to buy anything we want online with just one click. Add to this any poor money habits, like not tracking your money and not knowing what you're spending, and chances are you're not living within your means and you're on the road to extreme stress and high debt.

Along with "live within your means" is another long-time wealth principle: "pay yourself first." This means a portion of your money always goes to your investments and then what's left over is what you use to spend and pay your bills. This can be as easy as the example of taking $10 a month and putting it into an investment. People can easily find $10 a month by eliminating a lunch out or a couple of visits to a coffee shop. Small adjustments like these won't likely be missed by you but you will enjoy watching the $10 a month you put away grow. This also starts the habit of consciously putting money aside for you and seeing the impact a small amount can have overall. It will encourage you to keep adding to that $10 a month account. Once people get to this stage in their life, they're more comfortable and secure and they feel more independent. The reality is, until you have financial control, you're never truly free or independent, because you always have somebody to whom you owe money or somebody who has stake in your life or your family's life.

I always encourage people to get to the point where they are tracking their money and from there become disciplined about observing how money is coming in and going out. For instance, when you're shopping, start by pausing before each purchase. Ask yourself if you really need that item. If you do, can it wait until tomorrow? Next week? Impulses subside significantly over twenty-four hours, which means it's likely you'll wake up realizing you don't need that item after all—and you've saved yourself $20, $50, $100 because you didn't buy it on impulse.

By growing this muscle of discipline and observation, you will also begin to put every purchase into perspective. If you make $30 an hour and you want to buy something that costs $100, then consider how many hours you have to work to afford that item. Is it worth it to you to spend three hours plus on whatever it is? How important is that item when you make that decision?

These tips and spending practices work hand in hand with an effective budget. A budget is simply a way of tracking cash and expense flow. It tells you what money's coming, where it's coming from and where it's going. It's effective because it shows you where your money is going every month or every payday or every year, depending on how you do it. The shorter the time period that you track, the better, because then you can quickly make adjustments that need to be made. For example, if you are tracking your money every week, you will post your expense receipts and see where the cash was spent that week. Then every week or every second week, whenever your pay period is, you post where the money came in from, and you're always able to see if you have more money coming in than going out.

Over time, this observation will help you plan for the future. By knowing how much money you have coming in and going out, you can determine whether or not you can afford to buy a second car, take a vacation, or establish a good Christmas gift spending range. You'll also start to include the money you are setting aside for retirement. It will become a natural part of the cash tracking and will become a natural part of your lifestyle.

I've observed people with negative or fearful mindsets when it comes to their money and sometimes to budgeting itself. If you can stop thinking about budgeting as something that's tight and controlled, as though you have to track every single cent and you're not allowed to have your daily lattes anymore, you'll enjoy budgeting much more. Stop thinking about the words budgeting and restrictions. Just think that you're tracking your cash, which is all you're doing. You're seeing what you have. At the end of the day, or at the end of the month, the end of the week, whatever the term is, you'll have an idea of how much money you have coming in and going out of your house.

You'll feel a new peace of mind around money after only a few days of tracking how much is coming in and going out of the house. This is one of the biggest benefits of budgeting. The sooner you know how much money you can afford to invest and save for your future, the faster you can get started with it. The sooner you can start investing, the sooner you begin taking advantage of compound interest, where your money continues to grow by staying invested, and it is continually working for you. Investments have your money working for you all the time—your money is making money, basically. Many of the world's wealthiest people are significant investors, but it doesn't have to be – nor should it be – a secret, obscure activity designated only for the rich. Everyone with a dollar can invest, so get started and get your money working for you.

The other big benefit to having a budget is that as soon as you are clear about how much you owe to others, the sooner you can get it under control. The same compound interest that we love in investing is also at work in debt, only not in your favour. You're paying more all the time. It's easy to ignore, but if you just make minimum monthly payments on a credit card balance of $5000 at 21% interest, you're not paying your debt off: you're just paying the interest. The sooner you get a handle on it, the sooner you can fix it and the faster you can grow your investment money. This means you're now in control of your future and can control when and how you're going to retire and what kind of lifestyle you're going to have during your retirement.

People generally fail at budgets because they overwhelm themselves with trying to track every single item. Or perhaps they just don't get themselves in the habit of it or make it more complicated than it needs to be. By making it more complicated, they don't really know how to track the money. The easiest way to track your cash flow is to have a template and post your receipts every night or every week, depending on how many there are, into this template. Make it easy, do it while you're watching TV or during a few quiet minutes when you're off on your own. It's very simple to do and people fail to do it because they think it's more complicated than it really is.

The easiest way is to take a binder, draw a line down the centre of the page and on the left-hand side write the words "cash coming in" and on the right-hand side write the words "cash going out." Each night, record on the left- or the right-hand sides how the money flowed. If you want to use a computer and a program like Excel then you can download a budget template, or simply write the categories at the top of the spreadsheet, if you want more details. For example, you can have a category for Household Expenses, which are mortgage/rent payment, utilities, property taxes, telephone, etc. Then you can have a category Vehicle, and this would be lease/financing payment for your car, gas, repairs, insurance, and so forth.

Download a sample budget from **www.womenwise.ca**

Once you get started tracking what comes in and what goes out, you will want to graduate to adding categories for your expenses. You'll want to start analyzing where most of your cash is going and if there is anything you can do to hold on to more of it. The great thing about the budgeting or cash-tracking process is that it makes you aware of what you have and where it is going. This awareness leads to starting to take notice of what you are buying and seeing what you can do to be more efficient. I believe it happens naturally for everyone because once you start to consciously notice where your money is going you naturally want to keep more of it for yourself.

Another reason I think people fail at budgets is that they are afraid to know whether or not their money is flowing in the positive or negative direction. I think there's a lot of fear surrounding understanding money, so people avoid it more than they should. In reality, it's a lot easier to tackle something and get it under control so you know exactly where you stand than it is to ignore it, because ignoring it only makes it worse, especially if it's a debt situation. If it's not a debt situation and you're just afraid to know, then you're losing time that could be spent investing and accumulating compound interest on your investments. You're also subjecting yourself to a lot of undue stress by worrying about what you're trying to avoid.

The easiest way for someone to start a budget is to talk to somebody who is already a keen budgeter: a friend, a family member or a financial advisor. Or you can just download a template off the Internet. Don't be afraid to ask your advisor about this part of the plan. If they can't help you, chances are good they will know someone who can. There are lots of resources available. The hardest part is how to set up the right template for you, but don't get caught up with the details or format. Just download a template and start. Once you get started on it, you'll find out whether that particular template works for you and if it's missing columns or categories you need.

Budgeting is not something normally taught in schools, which is unfortunate, but it's never too late to start. There are books out there if you don't have a computer or the online space feels too big to wade into. You can certainly go to libraries or bookstores and get a book on budgeting and start to fill in the numbers. Just start to track it. Every time money comes into to your house, write it down. Every time money goes out, write it down. At the end of the period of either the week or the month, however you're tracking it, just subtract the cash in from the cash out and if it's negative, then look closer at what you're spending on. If it's positive, then you know you have money to invest and plan for future expenses.

If you don't know where to start at all when it comes to your money, budgets are a good first step. Building the muscle of tracking your money contributes to a solid financial foundation. Even if it's just noted in a notepad, the more you begin watching your spending habits, and seeing where your money is going, the more you'll recognize where you can make different choices. Your budget will inform how you spend over time, and it doesn't have to be restrictive at all. Whether your tracking shows a negative or a positive balance at the end of each month, this is valuable information and will help determine your next steps.

# Chapter 5

# Free Yourself from Debt

> *"I have about concluded that wealth is a
> state of mind, and that anyone can acquire
> a wealthy state of mind by thinking rich
> thoughts"*
>
> -Andrew Young

If you're reading this, there's a good chance you're among the high percentage of Canadians in debt. At the time of writing this book, 49% of Canadians live paycheque to paycheque and as I mentioned earlier, Canadians owe $1.71 for every $1 earned. In the case of the women I work with, the sad reality is that most of them have relied on somebody else to look after their finances for them. While this has typically been the tradition, they now find themselves in a position where they're single, either single again or single for the first time, even if they're single by choice. Couple this with the fact that there is not a lot of overt financial education available and it's no wonder women struggle with debt.

It happens easily, and it's nothing to be ashamed of. The typical trajectory for a modern woman is to finish college or university, get a job, spend at least forty hours a week working, get married, and raise a family. Who has time to study or learn more to become financially literate? Then, they're getting paid and spending money but perhaps not tracking it the way they should, and, before long, they're in debt.

Credit usually comes along at some point, and while it seems to be helpful, it's only temporary. Credit is basically someone extending terms to you to borrow money from them. When you get a credit card from MasterCard, Visa, American Express, or whatever the company is, that company is telling you how much they'll give you to spend, with the expectation that you'll pay them back either all at once or by paying a minimum monthly payment. To help you like this, the credit card company charges interest. A lot of people get trapped, however. It appears as though you can spend the limit and pay it back at your leisure, but by the time you pay back a card at $5000 with a 21% interest rate by making only the minimum monthly payments, for example $100, you'll have paid back over $7028 in interest!

Still, you need to have a credit card if you want to have a credit score, and credit scores are an essential piece of financial information in today's society. Your credit score is based on how much credit you have and how often that credit is revolving, if you're paying it on time and if there are any judgments against you. Your credit score is basically a snapshot of your financial situation as far as creditors are concerned. It's important because it is used as a determining factor when you go to buy a house or a car, for instance, or if you're trying to apply for another credit card. The bank, mortgage company, or car dealership will review your credit score to help determine what a suitable limit for you will be for a mortgage or car loan. They'll look at what your credit score is to see, first of all if you even qualify, and second of all, if you do qualify, what the terms are that you qualify for. The better your credit score, the lower your interest rate will be, usually.

A high credit score means you have good credit and therefore your interest rate should be good. If you have a lower score and you still qualify for a mortgage, for example, then you'll still get your mortgage, but you may not get it at the best rate that's available. This is why it's important to protect your credit and credit score.

Credit is also a determinant for lenders on a risk-versus-reward basis, so if your credit is good then their risk is lower, which means it's a reward for you. You get better terms of payment, lower interest rates, and more opportunities to get more money (if you're borrowing money) or a higher mortgage if you're buying a house.

It's a wise idea to check your credit at least once yearly. In Canada, you can check your credit once a year for free from credit companies like Equifax or TransUnion. Develop the habit of checking it so that you're always aware of the status of your credit. The other reason that you want to check it regularly is that if there's ever an issue of identity theft, it will show on your credit report and you can get it fixed sooner than later. The longer an identity theft goes unnoticed, the harder it is to fix your credit, and that will affect you in a negative way.

The biggest factors contributing to consumer debt, as I see it, are the concept of "retail therapy" and the easy availability of credit from retailers. Retail therapy is when we take ourselves shopping to get over a bad mood. This is fleeting, however. Still, for a vulnerable shopper, credit is very easy to get. Most major retailers have an in-house card or have offers that include discounts if you buy using their card. The retail industry has become a pro at making it very easy for people to buy now, pay later. Most people don't think of it, however, and 18 months comes faster than you think. If you're not prepared for it, problems arise. If you didn't have the money on the day of the purchase, it's likely you won't have it in 18 months either, especially if you didn't plan for it. The payments will include interest after that, and then become much higher.

Not having a plan to pay off any credit you are amassing is part of what sends you into debt. Making minimum payments is great for the credit card companies and even your credit score, but it's a slippery slope from making minimum payments on one retail store purchase to incurring greater debt that is out of control. This really is the primary cause of people getting into debt, in my opinion: the lack of education on how money works and how fast it can compound out of control in a negative way. It compounds in the positive way when you're investing it but it's important to understand just how fast it can get out of control in a debt situation.

We all need to be less concerned about what everybody else is thinking because the reality is most people are in debt. The person you're competing with, your next-door neighbour, your cousin, your brother, your sister, whoever it is, chances are high they're in debt, too. If they're not, well good for them. They are not the same age as you, they have different income circumstances and different family circumstances. You can't compete on an apples-to-apples basis with anybody. If people stop competing with others and only compete with themselves, they'll be in a better financial situation.

Solving the debt problem can feel overwhelming, and I see time and time again people believing they can't do it, they just can't get out of this mess. People who have a lot of debt, especially, rarely see the way out. They are still putting too much importance on money. While it's true that we need money for the rest of our lives, we don't need to put so much importance on it. Altering your relationship with money so that it's much more harmonious will help keep debt management stress at bay.

The big debts I commonly see, besides a mortgage, are credit card and student loan debts. Credit card debt especially doesn't add up overnight. It's like gaining weight and trying to lose it. It doesn't happen quickly. It takes time. If you don't know how to pay down the debt in a way that allows you to continue to put food in the fridge, it can feel like a monumental task. A lot of people give up because of this.

Paying down your debt, however, is just like any other big project that you have to do. Whether it's cleaning out your garage, your car, or the refrigerator, rather than continuing to avoid and walk past it, just tackle it one little bit at a time. It's amazing how good you will feel once the project is complete and, especially when it comes to debt, how much less stress and anxiety you will have. It feels good to be in a place where you can really start to save for your future and look after yourself.

The reality is, debt happens. Everybody will have debt at some point in our lives. Keep in mind, not all debt is bad. Any debt that is attached to an asset, like your mortgage, is considered "good" debt. How you handle and accumulate debt is important to consider, as someone with a higher level of financial literacy is able to leverage good debt.

People with a lot of money who have debt through mortgages are using other people's money to buy their second or third homes. They mortgage this home and use the money from the mortgage to invest, thereby making money off their money. On top of this, they're borrowing money from other people, so they're able to compound their net worth faster. This is one example of using good debt to our advantage. Consumer debt and student loan debt are considered "bad" debt and these are what need to be paid off. You need to develop a plan to pay them off sooner, rather than alter. A good plan will include debt payoff plus putting money aside for future investments.

The first thing I do with clients when we're talking about debt is write down a list of how much they owe and how much they have coming in. Then we put these lists together in a template and discuss the cash flow; what's coming in, what's going out. We do a budget together. Depending on how much debt some people have, I might do a "debt snowball roll-up" or calculation. This is a common debt pay-down approach, where you pay the same amount every month but you distribute the payments unevenly among the debt. For example, if you owe $100 on one card, with an interest rate of 21%, and you owe $500 on another card with a lower interest rate, say, 19%, and you owe $1000 on a third card with an even lower interest rate, then we might look at paying $300 every month and the first part will go to paying off the $100 or the card with the highest rate. Then, you continue to pay $300 every month until each debt is paid off.

If people are overwhelmed by budgeting as they pay down their debt, I try to do something easy. For instance, if they eat out a lot at a particular restaurant, I might put them on a program that will work for their budget while allowing them to continue eating there. I'll suggest they buy a gift card for $50 for that restaurant, and when it's done, they're done eating out. At the beginning of the month they can reload the card for another $50. This forces people to control their cash flow and budget without having to think too hard or be adding it up constantly.

By taking your budget seriously and taking the initiative to both get your debt down, and stay out of debt, ideally, you are avoiding any possibility of heading into a bankruptcy—and bankruptcy is a big deal and worth avoiding.

There is a stigma that is attached to declaring bankruptcy. Internally, you might feel a deep shame or guilt around it, while externally you risk losing respect from others, especially other business owners and people who persevered, worked with financial advisors, had a plan, and paid off their debt. Going bankrupt also does not guarantee you'll learn how to be financially independent and responsible, or how to save to invest and prepare for your future. It also doesn't help you avoid bankruptcy in the future. If you start out at a young age learning that bankruptcy just eliminates the debt and you get to start over, then you don't learn how to be financially responsible. You think that's the answer if you get into trouble again in the future.

I have a client who took on the debt of a family member at a very young age. Her credit was good, but theirs was not, so she took on their debt. She ended up declaring bankruptcy for them at the cost of her high credit score. The money that was owed had been spent for products and services that were not necessities. Her credit was racked up with items not required for daily living. A lot of debt gets incurred like this, from the need for getting something right away. Generations are learning from people who are just filing bankruptcy because they see their parents do it and thinking it all just goes away. The reality is that it's not easier, because a bankruptcy is with you for life. For instance, in Canada, you are not allowed to run for provincial or federal political office if you've had a bankruptcy. For credit purposes, you can expect to be asked about bankruptcy for five to seven years after your discharge. It can affect your career, too, as it is often a question asked by employers; whether it's been seven years or twenty-seven years since your bankruptcy ended, it could impact your chances of getting the job. You'll always have to declare it on any form that asks or be ready to provide the proof that your bankruptcy has been discharged. This doesn't mean you will be unable to do things you want to do; just be prepared that it is something that you will be asked about—in a financial, career, or any other context where a credit report is required—for the rest of your life.

If you have gone through a bankruptcy and you're getting back on track, you can start moving forward in a way where your money is working for you instead of fighting off debt. You can start by paying yourself first. You will have no more debt, so start by investing money and then making sure whatever is left over doesn't exceed what you need for expenses. Then you can get to work rebuilding your credit rating.

The best way to start rebuilding credit is to go out and get it. It's as simple as getting a credit card, even if it's just for $100. Get a small limit to start. Use it to buy gas and pay the balance off immediately so that it starts to rebuild your credit. Make sure that you don't start accumulating other cards and getting out of control again. Although I know most bankruptcy trustees have mandatory credit counselling sessions as part of the bankruptcy, I find it still doesn't teach you how to maintain your credit or make it better so you don't go through bankruptcy again.

You are focusing on rebuilding your credit, so don't get carried away. Don't get used to the credit card. Don't even carry the card in your wallet. Don't depend on the card. As a matter of fact, stick it in your freezer, stick it in the back of the drawer. If you don't have it on you, you won't be tempted to use it.

The upside of bankruptcy is that it eliminates your debt and gives you a free platform to start over with, without losing everything that you have. In Canada, you can have the tools of your trade exempt from bankruptcy, and your RSPs in some cases. There are ways to protect your other assets and investments from bankruptcy. It gives you the chance to start fresh with a clean slate and move forward, and if you're disciplined and you have a plan in place, this is very helpful. The problem with this is that if you don't fix your habits and your mindset and the discipline that you have with money, then you will just get yourself into that situation again. Essentially, your relationship with money has to change.

Every bankruptcy affects your credit. The more bankruptcies you have the harder it is to get credit. I have never encouraged somebody to go bankrupt. I think there's always a better solution than that. I also think there's an ethical part to it because you've already purchased goods and services and when you go bankrupt, those people are out the money owed. I understand that in some circumstances it may be the only way, but that is after all other options have been exhausted, including a consumer proposal.

The best way to avoid bankruptcy is getting your money situation handled, starting right now. By beginning to track your incoming and outgoing cash flow you're on your way to a budget that works for you. By managing how you use your credit cards and spending within your means, you will begin to incur less debt. If you already are in debt, don't get overwhelmed, and don't feel impatient. Believe me, taking the time to pay down your debt will feel more satisfying in the long run and offer you a lifelong experiential lesson in finance that bankruptcy sometimes fails to provide.

# Chapter 6:

# The Most Important Checklist I Have

> *"Old men are always advising young men to save money. That's bad advice. Don't save every nickel. Invest in yourself."*
>
> -HENRY FORD

 find that in general people don't have the same kind of excitement that I feel towards math, numbers, money and finances, so I created this financial to-do list to get you started. Starting is the biggest part, because I get it: this stuff can be overwhelming. You probably feel like you don't know where to start. My checklist removes any mystery and provides clear direction.

Regardless of how you process the information in this book, keep in mind the most important thing is not how much money you *make*, it's how much you *keep*. If you're spending more than you're making, it doesn't matter how much money you make. If you're not keeping enough of it, then you're not going to be able to have a secure future with your own savings and investments. This chart is an example of what a recommendation may be, the action plan, target dates and comments associated with it. It doesn't necessarily reflect a plan that fits everyone's financial needs. If you don't have kids, or debts, for example, those columns won't apply. If you have a cottage or vacation home, that would need to be added to this list. This is a basic checklist, adjust according to your specific situation.

| Recommendations | Action plan | Target dates | Comments |
| --- | --- | --- | --- |
| Get Home Equity Line of Credit (HELOC) to replace traditional mortgage, if fitting your financial situation | [insert actions] | [insert dates] | Completed |
| [Advisor Name] to meet with [Client name] and set up HELOC | | [insert dates] | |
| Once HELOC in place, pay off all debt (approximately $x) Set up Term 20 life insurance on Debt to replace mortgage insurance, if fitting your financial situation | [insert actions] | [insert dates] | |
| Set up RESP for kids, if fitting your financial situation | Make sure Government grants applied for (in Canada) | [insert dates] | |
| Set up [bank] account (get $50 bonus); use account to eliminate/reduce bank fees Once all debt paid: -Term 20 set up -RESP set up -Set up Tax Free Savings Act (TFSA) -Move $x from bank account to TFSA and invest | [insert actions] | [insert dates] [insert dates] | Must be done by [date], as that is end of $50 promotion |

This next checklist is a closer look at the first part of my financial to-do list. With this list, we're recommending ways to manage the money you have. I use this chart to help my clients identify what works for them, when it will be implemented, who needs to do the work surrounding the task and some narrative as to why it needs to be done or the benefit it will produce. Everyone can use this as a tool to very simply track what they need and want to do with their finances.

Let's start with the Home Equity Line of Credit (HELOC). This is basically a line of credit that is backed by your home. As it usually has an agreeable interest rate, you can use this line of credit for sizeable expenses, or to consolidate other loans with higher interest rates. If you are not eligible for a Home Equity Line of Credit, however, you can still get a traditional mortgage and set up the terms so that in one, three, or five years, whatever the case may be, you can transition to a HELOC without penalties. Typically, if done right, the HELOC will result in significantly less interest being paid than with a typical mortgage. However, it isn't for everyone. If you have discipline with your money and how you handle it, then you will be able to manage a HELOC. However, if you have always struggled with managing your money, a traditional mortgage might work better for you. Interest rates, your credit scores and other variables, including market conditions at the time you set your HELOC up, will affect how good a fit it is for you.

I had a client, Susan, who had two young kids and became single through divorce. Her husband left her with a big surprise of a lot of debt, some of which she didn't even know she had. When we started fleshing it all out and discovering all the places she owed and how much it added up to, it was very stressful for her. She was also working within a very tight time constraint. Her mortgage was coming up for renewal and she did not have the cash to pay off the debt that had to be paid off before the renewal date.

We got her pre-approved for a home equity line of credit and saw how much she would get and how that could work. She is actually very good and responsible with money; she just hadn't been looking after it. She made good money, had a good job, was a hard worker, and had a nice home. The interest rates on the debts were high and the home equity line of credit rates were much lower at the time (maybe 3%), so we used the line of credit to pay off the debts. Because I knew she was responsible and not a big spender, I was comfortable telling her we could do this because I knew she would keep paying the balance down on the line of credit, and that's what she's doing.

Susan's expenses included a mortgage insurance policy, which pays a level monthly payment on a decreasing value. That means you pay the same amount each month but the protection is actually decreasing in value because you are paying your mortgage off each month. If something were to happen to the insured, in this case Susan, the mortgage would be paid off, but no money beyond what was owed be given to her family. We looked at the premium she was pay-ing and realized that we could set up a term 20 life insur-ance policy, which lowered her current monthly payment. This policy was very, very inexpensive, and it covered the entire amount of the mortgage plus final expenses, and a little extra for the kids' higher education. We put that in place, and eliminated the mortgage insurance, which allowed her to save about half the cost. Basically, this plan allowed Susan to save money for the month.

In addition, it gave her 20 more years from the date we wrote the policy. This time frame matched with her new plan so she had the protection in place for the time that she needed it. With the small change we made, we saved her money on the monthly payment, and the life insurance policy will be paid out, in full, to her beneficiary (a family member), who can then decide what to do: either pay off the balance of the mortgage or make sure the children's education is paid for, or whatever else is required.

We set up RESPs for Susan's kids next because where Susan lives, in Ontario, Canada, she qualifies for a 20% government grant. This is part of the Canada Education Savings Grant program. It is an incentive offered by the government to save for your children's education. There is a grant of 20% on the first $2500 contributed to an RESP each year, or $500. There is a lifetime maximum and it is based on family income. I always encourage clients to look at applying for it, even if they don't qualify every year. If they qualify for the first few years, that's great, as it's basically free money that goes into the investment for the children's investment for their education.

We also readjusted Susan's banking because, like so many people, she was paying very high bank fees without even realizing she could avoid them. We got her set up with a new banking structure that allowed her to save a lot of money on fees. She wanted to begin investing, and, after this was all said and done, she ended up having a little bit of extra money come in. So we started a tax-free savings account (TFSA) for her investment.

Now, just as a note while we're discussing RESPs: someone who doesn't have children won't have a need for a RESP. However, they may have a charity they want to donate money to. In that case their action plan might be to take out an insurance policy to have in place with the charity as beneficiary, so when the time comes, it pays out and leaves their legacy. The options are endless but the right choices are specific for each individual.

We set the tax-free savings account to do double duty. This account is for long-term savings, usually for retirement. In Susan's case, she has it available as an emergency fund, or short-term savings, to help pay down some of the surprise bills that popped up the more we sorted through her finances. As we got through the plan, everything seemed to be settled down and we had everything sorted out, with this new flexibility of using the TFSA when things come up. Susan's TFSA is set up to invest in, so it's actually earning money. It's not just sitting in a bank account making nothing. It is also available for her long-term investments, if she doesn't need it in the short-term. Susan now has the comfort of knowing she is building up a "nest egg" if something transpires in the short-term, and if it doesn't then it will continue to stay invested, making money for her so that she has it in the long-term for retirement. Either way, it's a win-win for her. It also relieved a lot of her stress as she knew we were covering all the bases by using her money in a few different ways.

In Susan's case, she wasn't the one who got herself into financial trouble. If she had been the spender who got into financial trouble, then the home equity line of credit would have been a problem for her. If you don't have the discipline to not spend it when it's in front of you, you'll just continue to get in trouble. The home equity line of credit is a great tool for people like Susan because she was able to see that she could get everything sorted out and pay it down. Since it's a line of credit, you still have can use it if you need or want to. If you're a spender and you can't control yourself, however, you now have access to money that you could potentially blow on frivolous items.

The question is, what category are you in? Are you disciplined enough to handle having money in front of you and not spending it, or are you not disciplined at all? From my position, it's totally okay either way. As an advisor, I just want to have the honest information of my client's spending habits and mindset. Once I know that, we can put the right plan in place without me leaving any temptation in front of them. If Susan was the spender who got them into trouble, I would have looked at something else instead of a home equity line of credit so that she wouldn't have access to that money, thus keeping her out of trouble.

No matter your spending discipline, there is always a plan for you. I've helped people who knew they couldn't handle the HELOC. I've helped people who thought they could but I could tell they couldn't handle that strategy, so we did something different and they were grateful because I listened to them and worked with their true discipline. It is my job to listen, learn and put together an unbiased and honest plan for each person or family.

A lot of people are worried about telling the truth, especially when it comes to money, and it's essential that you're honest with your advisor. If you really are a spender, it doesn't serve you to lie because you're afraid of being judged. If you're a spender, there are still things that you can do to have a plan like this work for you to pay down your debt. I believe that a good advisor, asking the right questions, will know that. I also believe in making my office an environment where people feel safe to talk about their finances and know that there is no judgement. I don't believe in judging anyone because everyone has been through their own personal struggles and they have done the best they can with what they knew at the time. My job is to help get people to where they want to be.

I see women come in feeling embarrassed and scared, and they don't want to feel stupid. I know not to jump right in with questions about their financial status. I always make them comfortable, establishing the basics first. I ask them where they are, where they want to be, and what the difference is between the two. My job is to get a plan in place to move you from where you are to where you want to be. Once they get talking, they realize that my job is just to help them get on track. By that point, they're usually comfortable enough to say, okay well, here's what happened. Here's where I spent the money, this is how we got into this financial debt. Then it all comes together a lot easier, and a whole lot faster too.

Some women have issues with debt, while others might have a lot of money and they don't know how to invest it. It's all the same, however: where are you, and where do you want to be? How can we take this money and put it to the right use for you? It's the same thing, whether you want more money for traveling or for plastic surgery. The principles are the same. I just need to know the vision, and then I put the plan in place to get you there.

# Chapter 7

# Planning for the Future

*"A man only learns in two ways: one by
reading, and the other by association with
smarter people."*

-WILL ROGERS

Imagine you've gotten yourself to a place where your debt is under control (or gone entirely), your investments are in place, and your financial foundation is beginning to firm up. Now imagine having to cash in your investments because you became sick or injured. What happens if the illness or injury leaves you financially ruined with nothing left for the future? Good money management is not just about saving for the future, it's about making sure your financial foundation is strong and that you're financially protected. It goes beyond just saving for your future and your retirement, because if something happens and your savings get drained because of illness or accident, how much time do you have to replenish those accounts? It's likely you won't have much time, and this is where a good back-up plan comes in. This chapter explains a few simple ways you can look after yourself and your family and make yourself strong and healthy financially.

Barbara was a client of mine who ran her own business. She was single with no children, and her business was her life. When she came to me, I learned that she had been in a serious accident a few years prior, and that she had no disability insurance. She'd had the accident while on holiday, and spent a few years recovering. She knew that if she hadn't had her savings she really would have been in trouble. However, her recovery depleted her savings significantly. If she had paid her monthly premium on her disability insurance, she would have had income coming in without having to use up all her savings.

To talk with Barbara today is to talk to an advocate for disability or critical illness insurance. Consider what Barbara's options might have been if she hadn't had savings! Thankfully, she lives in Canada so most of her healthcare expenses were covered, although not items like her physiotherapy treatment. Had she lived in the US, however, she might have been bled dry just by the costs of treatment. It's easy to see how she could have incurred debt from the whole situation, which is a terrible way to get behind. Luckily, she had travel insurance which allowed her to receive treatment in the foreign country so she could return home, to Canada, to receive long-term treatment.

Barbara was still in her early forties when this happened, so she did what she had to do. When she came to see me, I prepared critical illness, disability, and life insurance policies for her. All of it ended up costing her $151 a month. These policies would provide her $25,000 in wellness and about $2500 a month for disability. Her life insurance was $250,000, and a portion of that cost her $65 a month. A portion of that within Universal Life (see below) went into the investment so it can grow for her for the next twenty years. This way, she could access that investment money in a very tax-efficient way.

All plans I create are custom-designed for the individual, keeping in mind what is important to them, how long they are planning to work, and similar factors. In Barbara's case, the living benefits of critical illness and disability were very important to her. She understood, first-hand, how life can change very quickly. In a case like Barbara's, where she has no partner or kids, the life insurance will go to pay the taxes for her business, and the rest she assigned to go to her parents should she die before them. When you get life insurance, you can decide who your beneficiaries are, and even what percentage would go to each. It doesn't have to be one beneficiary. In lots of cases, the beneficiaries are split between people and even a portion is assigned to a charity.

A lot of people balk at the concept of critical illness insurance, seeing it as "just one more bill." But if I were to tell you that in the event of an accident or illness, you can have a lump sum, tax-free, no strings attached cheque handed to you, won't that make your life a little bit easier? Wouldn't it make your family's life a little bit easier? If you get diagnosed with a life-threatening illness and a family member has to take time off work to take care of you and help you get to your appointments, is it helpful to add stress and worry about finances to the situation? Not at all. You know you still have to pay for your house. You have to pay your taxes. You have bills to pay. The expenses still exist, and what critical illness insurance does is alleviate the stress of meeting those expenses so that you can focus on getting well.

Believe it or not, critical illness or disability insurance is not, necessarily. very expensive. It's also not painful and it doesn't hurt your feelings. You don't have to talk about it all the time. All you have to do is take comfort in knowing that you have something in place and if something ever happens, you are taken care of. At its core, critical illness or disability insurance is meant to replace your income were something to happen to you.

Life insurance, however, is *not* about estimating and paying into a policy that reflects what your life is worth. After all, how much is your life worth? It doesn't matter what formula I give you when it comes to determining how much life insurance you need. It's based on measurable dollars and cents, but how can you measure what your life is worth? How much does it cost to replace you? Is it $5000? $100,000? $1 million? $100 million?

The truth is, life insurance is about putting in place what you actually need for your family when the time comes that ensures they'll be looked after and left without stress or discomfort. Simply put, making sure there is no other hardship for the family (beyond your illness or injury) is what life insurance offers. There's certainly nothing wrong with leaving your family financially comfortable, even better off, in some cases. No matter how much financial coverage you have, it will never replace you to your family. But you'll make it easier for them to grieve you without worrying about the financial stress.

Life insurance can act like the great ATM of the family when you're no longer there. It gives you a payout for your children and, if your spouse is still around, life insurance substitutes for your income while your spouse figures out childcare and the family expenses after you're gone. Sometimes the spouse needs time off, too, depending on how many children there are and how the childcare is structured. Sometimes it costs more for people to have their kids in childcare than it does for a parent to stay home. If that's the case, then life insurance substitutes for the missing income. Life insurance on you doesn't benefit you: it benefits whomever the beneficiary is.

Ideally, you want your life insurance to do two things for you. First, you want it to leave money in place for your family so that if you are not there to cover bills, expenses or debt, these will be covered. Second, you want to use your life insurance as a vehicle through which you pass wealth onto the next generation.

I encounter a lot of people wondering whether they need life insurance. Well, if you have kids and two incomes and something happens to one of those incomes, you will need life insurance to cover your debt and your children's education. It also needs to cover any income replacement because it is quite an adjustment to go from two incomes to one. This is part of the calculation as you figure out how much life insurance you need. Basically, how much life insurance you need is based on how much you have in debt and how much you want to either leave for your children's education or leave to a charity (if you are single or don't have children). Determining how much life insurance you need is really just a simple numbers game, and a process you can also do with an advisor.

> **Here is a simplified list you can quickly do right now to figure out how much insurance you need:**
>
> **1.** Total Debt
>
> **2.** Income replacement
>
> **3.** Mortgage amount
>
> **4.** Final expenses
>
> **5.** Children's education
>
> The total of the above five items is roughly the amount of life insurance you need.
>
> For more detailed information and for access to insurance calculator, visit my website **kathycooknoble.gpwealth.ca/**

There are both permanent and temporary life insurance products available. As you may have guessed, a permanent policy means a policy that is in effect even if you live to be 100 or 150 years old. It doesn't matter: the policy is in place, the term never expires. A temporary or term life insurance policy is one with an expiry date.

In Canada, permanent insurance also gives you the option to hold investments in it. This means you can invest your money, but you also have access to that money, which is called its "cash surrender value." This kind of insurance policy also offers growth on the investment side, with some tax efficient qualities. Among the permanent insurance plans available are Whole Life and Universal Life insurance. In simple terms, Whole Life policies have fixed premiums, which means you pay the same amount every year, while Universal Life premiums are flexible, which lets you adjust what you pay each year by dipping into the cash value of the policy. You still have to pay a minimum premium amount, however.

If you are investing money inside the policy, chances are you have a Universal Life policy. In this case, you contribute money to the investment side so you can actually grow your money—and grow it before taxes. There is also a very tax efficient way to withdraw money out of your policy, which makes it good for tax planning, too. It's similar to an RRSP in that it's tax deferred growth. The investments are able to grow, you are able to access them, if needed, and you can do this while being very tax efficient. Of course, there are restrictions on how much you can put into the investment and how much you can take out, and when. Still, depending on the size of the policy and face value, you can contribute quite a bit of money. You can grow money in the investment, and then withdraw it so that you have it and it becomes part of your tax planning for retirement. Whatever is left over is part of your estate. This is something you have to set up with your advisor and decide if it is part of your financial plan. As with all investments, they are specific to the individual or family and I strongly recommend talking to an advisor to set up a plan that is right for you.

The investments that you can use in the Universal Life or Whole Life policies are good investments. In fact, they are as good as or sometimes even better than investments outside of an insurance policy. You are not sacrificing your quality of investment by having it inside an insurance policy. At the end of the day, one is not necessarily better than the other; it's always case dependent. It's not any better to have an investment outside the policy than it is to have inside the policy. Not everyone needs this kind of insurance, either.

Temporary insurance, or term insurance, is a policy issued for a specific length of time. For example, a Term 10 is a 10-year policy. Typically, if it's a Term 10, the rate will remain exactly the same every month for 10 years and if you don't pay it the insurance gets cancelled, period. It's basic, simple, and straightforward. It's usually inexpensive and it's almost always the way to go for covering your mortgage.

As a quick side note, when it comes to covering your mortgage, there is also mortgage insurance. With mortgage insurance, you pay a fixed amount every month which covers only your mortgage. You will then have a reducing debt on your mortgage because it goes down each month that you pay it. Thus, every time you make your mortgage insurance payment you're paying the same amount of a monthly payment but you're actually getting less coverage. Also, mortgage insurance typically gets paid to the person who holds the mortgage so the money doesn't go to your family. This is why it might make more sense to choose a term policy that is then directed to your family and have that term policy for the length of time of your mortgage. This way, you pay the same amount of money each month, and the money is directed to your beneficiary if something happens to you. The beneficiary becomes the one to decide whether or not to pay off your mortgage. There is no law stating that your mortgage must be paid off if you die.

Life insurance contracts are generally easy to read and understand because they are typically based on a standardized document. With life insurance, you are reading a contract, not a statement. It would only be a statement if there was an investment component to it, which in Canada is only under the Whole Life and Universal Life policies. Otherwise, it is an insurance contract, which shows you the following:

- Date you bought it
- Company you got it from
- Person who is insured (presumably that's you)
- Named beneficiary (who gets the money when you die)
- Coverage amount (what's the face value of the payout, which could be $100,000 or $1 million or something else)
- Term of the policy (how long it is good for)

Your contract will also tell you if it's a renewable policy, which means it will renew every year at whatever the annual premium rate is. It will tell you if it's convertible, which means you can convert it from a term policy to a permanent policy, like Whole Life or Universal Life.

Take a close look at your coverage summary when reviewing the contract; you want to see exactly what you're covered for. For instance, you want to make sure it's not a life insurance policy that only pays out if you die on a Thursday. You won't be around to fight for your policy, so make sure you've got the right one! The coverage summary will tell you the following:

- Who's covered
- What they're insured for
- What age they're insured to
- If it's a permanent life or term policy
- If there are any riders on it (you can add riders to a policy to cover critical illness, for example, or children)

I cannot emphasize enough the importance of knowing your policy. Another advisor once shared with me that they had a client come in and buy a policy, and they never saw the person who sold it to them again. The client had been paying automatically for 10 years when they came into my advisor friend's office. It's typical to not see your advisor every year, and particularly if all that advisor sold was life insurance. However, you should review your policy frequently. If you have another child, or you want to convert the policy, or add more, it's important to consider regularly checking in with the advisor. Remember your circumstances change over time and so, too, may your insurance needs. In the case of this client, they thought they were insured so the advisor offered to review it for them.

As my advisor friend reviewed the policy, they saw something that caught their eye. "You must ride the subway a lot," the advisor commented. The client, surprised, said, "We never take the subway." The advisor then had to tell the client that the policy would only pay out if they died on the subway in Toronto.

Although it was fortunate that the client discovered that before dying, they had been paying for it for 10 years. That meant the cost of the premium was higher as they were now 10 years older than when they first purchased the policy.

If it's a straight term policy, not convertible, that means you can't change it into something else. If it is, you can transfer it into a permanent policy, and add or subtract insurance coverage. It just depends on how the policy is written, and who the company is. Don't be afraid to ask a professional advisor to review the policy you have or are considering and help you make sure you have the right coverage for you and your family.

If you have kids, you may also want to consider getting children's life insurance. Children's life insurance is not essential, however there are a few useful reasons to get it. First, it's usually a lot less expensive because they're young. Second, it pre-qualifies them for insurance in the future. If they come into a health issue when they're older and they already have life insurance, then they're pre-qualified and it can't be taken away from them. If the child becomes epileptic, or has some kind of disease at age 18, that can affect the premium rate on life insurance. If they already had life insurance as a child, the rate will not be affected.

I don't normally recommend people solely rely on life insurance covered through a group plan that's paid for by the employer. This is because unless you pass away during your employment, it's not going to pay out. The plan is typically going to end once you retire. At that stage in your life it could be very expensive to get your own policy, or you may not qualify for coverage. I encourage people to confirm if the policy ends with employment. We also take a look at what is covered under the company's policy (i.e. how much, terms, etc.) and then come up with a plan that supplements any deficiencies. This way the individual is covered for what they actually need, so when they retire, they have a small plan of coverage that is already in their name. Review your group benefits with your advisor to make sure they fit your overall financial plan, and fill in any holes or deficiencies.

Along with life insurance there are disability insurance, long-term healthcare and critical illness insurance options. In my opinion, everybody needs to be covered for disability somehow. If a client has group insurance and they're covered under disability, I always ask them to check and see what they're actually covered for and for how long.

Disability can be very expensive if you're not prepared. Typically, the amount of disability insurance a person needs is around 60% of their salary. Most disability insurance provides a tax-free benefit, so 60% of tax-free income is pretty close to 100% of taxable income. There is a maximum limit to the coverage, and it's certainly not a reward, it's pay for when you are out of work. Disability insurance does what it's meant to do—help you get well so you can go back to work. The good thing about disability insurance is that you don't use it and lose it, you can always use it again. For instance, if you're a plumber and you break your wrist, causing you to be unable to work, then after you've recovered and gone back to work you still have your disability insurance in place. This means even if you don't get hurt for another 10 years, you can still go back to your disability insurance and get some help. At the end of the day, disability insurance really is there to help you.

I also believe everyone should have critical illness insurance. The difference between critical illness and disability insurance is that with critical illness insurance you receive it as a one-time lump sum payment, after which the policy is over and you stop paying your premium. Contrast this with disability, which is like getting a monthly income, where the benefit ends when you get back to work. With critical illness, the benefit ends once you get the cheque.

The statistics of people getting cancer are so much higher now that it's clear critical illness insurance is essential. It helps you get through the health scare with the least amount of financial disruption that you could possibly have. It gives you peace of mind knowing that you don't have to drain all your finances just to keep afloat. Critical illness insurance offers security: people know they're covered so they can focus on their health and recovery. I recommend people talk to their advisor to see if critical illness insurance fits their financial plan.

There are also life insurance policies that are a combination of life insurance with critical illness. This is very helpful, because a policy like this allows you to borrow money off the face value of the policy. Actually, it's not even borrowing, because you actually get the money at the face value of the policy while you are ill. You pay for your insurance plan and you can pull money if you are diagnosed with one of the illnesses that you're covered for. In other words, you have a guaranteed life insurance plan still in place, and you can use part of the premium as critical illness if you need it. This adds another layer of protection as well as peace of mind.

Buying life insurance usually gets us thinking about our mortality, and beyond just life insurance, it's essential that you get your will prepared. In the next section, we will discuss what you need to know about wills.

## Preparing A Will

Everyone has an estate, whether or not you think you do. Just because you rent your apartment and don't own a car doesn't mean you don't have an estate. Your dog, your cat, your grandma's fine china that you want to pass on: all of these are part of your estate. Further, if you have a favourite niece or nephew you want to pass things on to, you'll have to get your estate in order, otherwise the government will step in once you're gone and they have their own way of divvying up the goods—which is not *your* way! This means your favourite niece or nephew might not get anything because you haven't properly laid out your plans for your estate.

Having a will covers all your assets. In a sense, it covers tax-paying as well. It looks after your final wishes and makes sure your estate (i.e. stuff) gets handled and distributed the way you want it done. It gets the momentum started so you can feel successful that you've taken the first step and gotten something accomplished.

Your estate is also about when you're here. There is something called a "living trust" that you may want to set up if you want to pass the family business onto your children while you're still alive. Doing this means any future capital gains will be taxed on their account, rather than on yours. This is a great way to do estate planning for family businesses. This will need the help of your advisor, lawyer and accountant to set up.

Having your will in your financial plan is also helpful. Regardless of how you work it into your financial plan or keep your will separate, don't be daunted—wills are actually easy to do. While they can be done by a lawyer, it's not necessary; you can prepare your will yourself. If you have young children, you need a will so that they are looked after; protect your family by protecting your kids. The bottom line is, you need a will so that the government is not poking around in your affairs when you are no longer here.

All estates are subject to some kind of estate administration tax, depending on where you live. Each province is different in Canada. This happens with or without a will. In Ontario, the Estate Administration Tax is the tool that the government uses to calculate how much tax is owing. This tax replaced probate fees, and is calculated on the total value of the person's estate. That means all their belongings, including investments, are added together and the amount of tax is calculated. Whether you have a will or not, when you die the Canada Revenue Agency (CRA) or Internal Revenue Services (IRS) are going to tax your estate as if you had sold all your capital property. Your stocks, your business, your real estate, everything that you own with the exception of your family home becomes something that the CRA looks at to determine how much tax they are owed. Your primary residence may be exempt from capital gains and may be transferred to a beneficiary tax-free, so it is usually better to hold your principal residence jointly with your spouse or your partner and that way it bypasses your estate and any probate fees and goes directly to him or her. Everything else, however, gets put in a pot and its worth determined. Then they add it up and figure out how much tax is paid on it. As a result, your estate may actually end up with a big tax bill that might have to be paid by selling some valued assets.

There are ways to be more tax efficient with your estate, and to help minimize any estate taxes you have to pay. The will states your wishes, and the financial plan helps with litigating the estate tax, so more of the estate gets to your family or charity or to whom you wish. A good financial plan will ensure that more will stay with you than will go to tax. You should look at what's available to minimize the tax obligation. This should also be reviewed periodically to make sure any changes in the law or your net worth are addressed.

Regardless of the size of your estate, everyone needs a will. Everyone deserves to have their final wishes executed and not left to interpretation. If it's not written down, there's no binding proof it's really what you want. For instance, you might have a family heirloom that you want to make sure goes to a specific person, and even if you verbally tell them that, there's no written proof after you're gone. The will is your final note to everybody to say what you want, how you want it, and how you want it done.

Having a will eliminates fighting between family members by removing all opportunities for misinterpretation. It eradicates the heightened emotional state people sometimes get into when trying to think of something rational or recall what you said. A will is simply a legal document that is to be implemented, thereby getting rid of any need for discussion. Of course, there are specifics as to how the will gets written up, the length of the will and other details to pay attention to. If a person owns a business, for example, they will likely need more assistance with their will, depending on the size of the business, if it's incorporated, and so on. It may have more pieces to manage than a person who does not own a business. Whatever the case may be, they all need a will.

Preparing your will ensures that your estate is managed the way you want it to be, because you certainly don't want the government to interpret it for you (which is their legal right to do if you die without a will). If your assets are not allocated specifically in a will, the government steps in and they decide how things get divided based on blood relations, whether or not you're married and your spouse is still alive, and whether or not you have kids. If your spouse is still alive, a specific amount will automatically be assigned to them. Assuming that your spouse has died and the property is being distributed to the children or a charity, if you don't specifically say you want the money to go to a charity, there's no obligation for that to happen. Also, everything has to go through probate, so you may have to pay probate fees, and these can be quite expensive. The probate rules are different in each jurisdiction, which means sometimes it's cheaper to die in a different province or country!

As I mentioned earlier, your estate is not only relevant once you're gone; it's also something to consider when you are here. Gifting is one way of reducing the value of the probate-able estate. Gifting basically reduces the amount that can be taxed when you die because you're giving it away while you're alive. Gifting when you're still around allows you to also see the joy and happiness of the people that you're giving it to while you're here. Gifting is one of the great ways that you can take advantage of tax planning and tax efficiency, as well as some emotional planning and efficiency.

Another aspect of will preparation is choosing the right executor. You want to pick someone you trust and like and who you know will have the best interest of everyone in mind when it comes time to execute your will. Being an executor is quite a responsibility, as they are the last connection to the final wishes of the will holder. The roles and responsibilities of the executor are all drawn up in the will, which is a legal document, so there is some accountability built into the role. The executor's tasks include locating the will and reviewing it for specific funeral arrangements, helping with the arrangements, and getting multiple copies of the death certificate and the will, so that all parties involved have one. It's helpful to have a trustworthy ally as your executor and it will give you peace of mind knowing your wishes will be implemented once you've gone.

Despite common misconceptions, preparing a will is neither complicated nor costly. As I mentioned earlier, while you can have your will prepared by a lawyer, you can actually prepare your will on your own. If you want to build your will into your financial plan, however, be aware that financial advisors don't prepare wills. If you decide to prepare your will yourself, there are kits available that you can use. There are different software programs that you can buy, such as LegalShield, which offers a pretty decent membership. You can get a standard will done through them at a really affordable price. Most people only need a standard will; nothing complicated like what I went through. Once you've prepared your will, just get it signed and witnessed by people who will not be beneficiaries of it.

## Power of Attorney and Health Care Directive

In addition to a will, be sure to prepare a Power of Attorney and a Health Care Directive. A Power of Attorney is a document that states who is appointed to be in charge of your financial matters if something happens to you—for example, you end up in a coma—and you are not able to handle your financial affairs. If you are unable to pay your mortgage, property taxes, etc., they still need to be paid, so make sure there is someone in charge of handling that for you until you can do it again yourself.

If you don't appoint a Power of Attorney, you risk having the government step in, via public trustee, and take over your accounts, your investment portfolio, and all your assets without consulting your family. The rules on how this works vary from province to province in Canada, and from state to state in the US. You want to have this in place because you don't want there to be any guesswork. Having a Power of Attorney is to help you while you're alive in the event that you become incapacitated somehow and it has left you in a position where you are unable to deal with your finances.

A Health Care Directive is similar to a Power of Attorney, only this involves putting someone in charge of your medical decisions. Make your intentions clear should something happen to you: for example, can you receive a blood transfusion, is CPR okay, and so on. This person is responsible for administering your wishes while you are unable to.

These two additional documents are straightforward, easy to get done, and will have a profound impact on your life if needed. These are the documents that help people help you while you are alive and need the help but are unable to arrange it yourself. Do these documents when you do your will, so that you are protected in all areas.

If you're reading this at age thirty and in a panic, I want to reassure you that you can still get this done even if you don't do it today. Regardless of how old you are, there is always something you can do. Sometimes people don't get around to estate planning until their 70s. In Canada they were told to pay off their mortgage and invest in their RRSPs (Registered Retirement Savings Plans). RRSPs might be similar to 401Ks in the U.S. For many of these people, they're only just realizing that RRSPs are taxable. Now they try to do some estate planning and make sure more goes to their family rather than taxes and probate fees.

I had a client come to see me at the age of 72. He had RRSPs and wanted to update his will, which hadn't been updated for thirty years. Because of his age we had less flexibility on what we could do or products we could access. Although he also had a life insurance policy in place, it wasn't enough to cover all the taxes that were expected to be owing. Still, it was all I could do with him at first, and it made the most sense, cost-wise. He had already converted his RRSPs to RRIF (Registered Retirement Income Funds) because he was 72, and these have to convert at age 71. At 71, you have to begin withdrawing and paying some of the tax. He was just taking the minimum when I saw him. He didn't have a Tax-Free Savings Account (TFSA), but he did have some extra money which we put into a TFSA as an investment. This way, he could grow that money, tax free, for the next 15 years or however long he lives.

In Canada, general life expectancy statistics show men living to 85 and women to 87, so my client needed at least another 10 or 15 years' worth of money. He did have that at the time, but if he had been pulling it all out of his Registered Retirement Income Fund (RRIF), it would have been 100% taxable. He had a Universal Life policy, so we were able to do a little bit there, although not a lot because there wasn't much time for us to put money in and let it grow. He wanted to make sure his grandchildren would be looked after. He wanted life insurance on his grandchildren because he did that on his kids when they were younger. We did a life insurance policy on his grandkids and we also started an investment for them.

Then we talked with his kids so that everybody knew what was going on. He wanted to divide his assets very evenly, so we divided the estate by the number of kids and then considered if any of the kids wanted the family home. If so, what was the value of the house, and how do we transfer that to that particular child while making it even for the other children? We made sure he knew what he had, how much it was worth and that it was very fair for all three kids.

I always tell people to start now, but even if you're older there's always something you can do, no matter what your age. There is a lot more you can do at 20, and there's still a little bit you can do when you're in your 70s. It just gets harder and more expensive if you're going to use any product in terms of life insurance. It requires different planning.

Once you have your firm foundation of budgeting or at least tracking your money, you are setting yourself and your family up for the future by adding life insurance and a well-prepared will. These are a big part of your financial legacy, and the ultimate in planning for the future.

# Chapter 8:

# How Money Grows

*"We must all suffer one of two things: the pain of discipline or the pain of regret or disappointment."*

-Jim Rohn

Would you believe it if I told you that it's actually fun to save? You can make it fun and you can make it fun as a family, too. If you're getting your money in line as a mother, and sharing with your kids, it's not taboo to talk about how you're planning and saving for vacation. Or to suggest that instead of buying gifts for the kids at birthday time you buy one small gift and put the rest of the money into a vacation fund. Doing it as a family and talking about it makes it fun.

I see a lot of people who think saving takes work or think there's something they don't understand about it. These are the same people who think financial people are speaking a foreign language, using acronyms, metrics, benchmarks. The reality is you can understand it in plain language. It's always a challenge learning new things, and it might not be all that much fun in the process. Learning to ride a bike isn't necessarily fun at the time, but once you know how to ride, it's a lot of fun. It's the same with finance; watching money grow and seeing all you can do with the money you are growing is fun. If you're passionate about animals and love dogs, you can save money and donate to an animal rescue and help save dogs. Do good things with your money, and you'll start seeing how saving is fun.

In the moment, it feels like you're giving something up, or you have to sacrifice your quality of life. In reality, we always have pain in our lives, and we often have to make sacrifices. I like how entrepreneur Jim Rohn puts it: we either have the pain of discipline or the pain of regret in our lives, but either way, pain is there. If you're disciplined and save your money you may experience the pain of discipline, but you'll have the reward of a well-funded retirement. Consider the opposite, where you spend throughout your life, only to find yourself at 70 with the pain of regret that you didn't save all that time.

It's fun to save with your family, and it's even more fun to save when you're single! Imagine saving to buy your own home, or a Tesla. Or imagine you're a nurse, and it means a lot to you that the hospital you worked for could have a mammogram machine or MRI, and you're the one who can leave that to them as part of your legacy. How cool is that? While you're alive, you can save money that you can then give back to the community through donations, sponsoring a family, or helping needy kids have Christmas. The fun of it comes from knowing your future is taken care of, you have security, yet you can live the lifestyle you want and pay it forward. It is always fun to make somebody feel better or feel good about something. People feel good giving time and money. Philanthropy has a lot going for it. It starts with being disciplined and saving.

If you feel overwhelmed just by the thought of saving, take a deep breath. Start by writing down your goals, then look at them realistically and prioritize. Some savings goals might overlap: for instance, an emergency fund is not necessarily unrelated to a retirement fund, it could be both. Or another fund could be travel and fun money. You don't need to look at setting up ten different accounts to start saving with; maybe consider three that have objectives that work together.

A good first place to find money to save is with your bank fees. The average Canadian pays $15-$20/month to their bank as a basic account fee, and this isn't including overdraft or any other charges. If you switch to a no-fee, or low fee, bank account, you could start putting what you would have paid in fees straight into your savings.

There are a few no-fee banking options for people living in Ontario. Tangerine, is an example no-fee banking. The Big 5 banks in Canada are beginning to expand and buy smaller banks in both Canada and the U.S. The Big 5 banks each average $2 billion quarterly, a $60 billion profit combined in 2016. Good financial planning helps you keep that money for yourself. The money you have been spending in fees can be redirected to investments and savings or paying down debt. As I said earlier, the most important thing is not how much money you make, it's how much you keep.

A great place to start with savings is to have an emergency fund. With an emergency fund, you are in a much stronger place to determine your future. You have much more choice when something happens. While it may seem unnecessary when you're a vital young woman in good health, everyone needs an emergency fund. Emergencies are not just health related. Sometimes the car has major repairs needed, or you have to make a sudden return flight home from a vacation because something has happened, or you lose your job. These are all emergencies.

If nothing else, having your emergency fund shows that you are the one deciding your future. You're the one in control of your finances. If you don't have control of your finances, then you don't have financial freedom—and by financial freedom I mean affording your life without depending on anyone else. If you don't have financial freedom, you don't actually own your life. After all, until you're financially free, you're not free, because you always owe something to somebody. I believe it's important for people to have a complete sense of autonomy when it comes to their lives and the decisions they make.

Think back to the beginning of the book. We met Anne, who had debt from her student loans but still loved to shop and go out with her colleagues; and then we met Jessica, who was much more prudent with her financial choices. For a lot of us, life rolls out quite similarly. We get out of university and the world is one big opportunity, so we feel excited. We may have a hard time getting the job we really want, so we work at a job that's not exactly what we want. Further, that job has a boss who doesn't treat us with a lot of respect; our time is not valued. We can't afford to leave because we need money to pay for our home or car. It's a vicious cycle, one choice leading to the next, and it's a quick spiral to despair if we're not careful.

What if we could all be like Jessica, though? What would it take to buy cheaper food, drive a cheaper car, make the sacrifices we need to make in order to put savings into an emergency fund? By doing this, if the boss doesn't like you, you have more choices. You can quit. If you get harassed by a senior employee, you can leave because you're no longer desperate for money. You have your emergency fund. If your relationship turns sour and you have to leave it, you will have the money for first and last month's rent on a new place. All because you chose to save. Nobody controls you but you. That's what choosing to save is about.

I speak from experience. Thinking back to the story I shared earlier, if I hadn't had savings when everything went down with my family and the succession plan, I'd have been in big trouble. I went almost a year with no pay! My parents refused to even pay my wage while I was still working there getting this sorted, and it wasn't even a big wage to begin with. I'd accepted a low salary because I'd been promised the business. They hadn't paid out Employment Insurance for me, either, because I was considered an "owner." This meant that when they stopped paying me altogether, I had access to nothing. I had no pension plan. I had no pension. If I hadn't been saving and doing my own investing I'd have been desperate, and even worse, would not have had my family to turn to for support.

Whether you believe you can choose to save or not, I'm telling you that even today, even if you're in debt, you can start saving. Your independence, your autonomy, your freedom, all of these are what's at stake when you don't have a commitment to saving. Aren't you worth putting a few dollars away each month?

# Chapter 9:

# Investing for Beginners

*"Self-reliance is the only road to true freedom, and being one's own person is its ultimate reward."*

-Patricia Sampson

There is saving and then there is investing. What's the difference, really? I think of investing as a long-term savings option; in an investment, your money is committed, and it's usually more difficult to withdraw it. A savings account is used for a specific event or time, like saving for a wedding, a graduation, or a motor home. Our investment accounts are left for the long term, and we watch them grow over a period of time.

Before I get into the nitty-gritty of investing, I want to touch on the common streams of investing. There is investing in your retirement fund, which is my primary focus, and there is also real estate.

As an investment, real estate is great if you do it right, but many people fail to account for the real costs of buying and selling a property. If you are planning on making money in real estate and using it as an investment, you really have to understand and account for the costs associated with it. Most people think they buy a property for X amount and sell it for Y amount and their profit is the difference. They forget, however, to take into account all the of other expenses found in-between; the closing costs, carrying costs, realtor fees, and so on. One of the most common mistakes I see is people also not factoring their time into these costs, either. If you are planning to do renovations, upgrades, painting, or any of the work required to raise the value of a property yourself, it costs your time. Don't undervalue that!

I tell my clients to compare apples to apples. You have to know what the real rate of return is going to be on the investment, and on the real estate, which means the net of all costs. Real estate is also similar to investments in that it is dependent on how the market is doing as well. For instance, at time of print, Canada has just been through an incredibly hot real estate market, and the government has done some things to cool it down a little bit. This is done through interest rate hikes and making mortgage qualifications more difficult. They do this to control the growth in the market.

As I have been saying throughout the book, it's important to have all your facts and then make the best choice for you, and that includes understanding the market, interest rates, and all the factors involved.

Another question to ask yourself if you are considering investing in real estate is: how long do you plan on holding the property? A lot of people think they can just take one of those real estate courses and get rich quick but there's quite a bit of work to it, and you have to have money to put down. You have to either have the funds or you have to be able to access funds, either through a line of credit or mortgage. While lots of people have certainly made a lot of money in real estate, there are just as many who went broke because they didn't have all their costs figured out, and they didn't have all their information lined up.

Real estate is not a surefire thing. Some people get confused and think that real estate is an easy guarantee and it's not. I know a lot of developers that have gone bankrupt because they didn't account for their holding costs, and they didn't account for how much it was going to take to actually get the property ready for re-sale so they could actually make money. As a general rule, I never give advice to my clients about which lot or property to buy because it is tough to do that without seeing the whole picture.

As a financial advisor, I work with investments that are low, medium and high risk After performing a risk profile I am able to recommend what is appropriate for each individual person or business. That includes recommending certain types of investments; such as mutual funds, ETFs, segregated funds, etc. Each recommendation Is custom to each Individual.

If real estate makes you nervous, or is not your thing, investing may be a more suitable option for you.

While I specified above that investments are usually left to grow over a period of time, you can invest with a shorter time commitment. It depends on what kind of advisor you are working with. As I mentioned earlier in the book, some advisors are fee-based, and others work on commission. If you are working with an advisor who is paid on commission, then you are often committed for a certain amount of time because there will likely be penalties for early withdrawal. Either way, for an investment to really grow, it needs the time to be invested and allow the magic of compound interest to happen.

Depending on how you arrange things, your savings could still be invested, but they just might be invested for a shorter period of time. Your long-term investments could be committed to a longer term because it doesn't matter if they are subject to a penalty; the penalty drops off after a certain number of years, and you aren't going to be withdrawing anyway within the few years the penalty might exist.

The job of the advisor is to look into various funds and companies and understand the performance of the portfolio manager. A quality advisor is good at choosing funds and knowing their fees and past performance, the fund manager, and the fund risk, all while keeping in mind your personal goals, your age, and what you are seeking to build from your investments. Ideally, they're taking into account your politics and morals, if that is important to you. There's a big swing towards ethical investing nowadays, and people who care about the environment certainly don't want to invest in projects or companies that violate their morals and ethics. There are plenty of publicly traded companies whose missions and ethics line up with a concerned and conscious investor. Investing ethically is not a sacrifice of your money. If your advisor is unaware of sustainable companies, you can do the research and present the results to them.

Where to begin with investing? I like to start with the acronyms: RRSPs, RRIFs, RDSPs, RESPs, and TFSAs (don't worry, I explain these below in more detail). When I used to teach this to college students, I would joke that any investment that started with an "R" meant the "R" stood for "rules." For instance, an RRSP is a Registered Retirement Savings Plan, and that first "R" (meaning "Registered") really meant rules, because rules go with anything that is registered. All these acronyms, "R"s or not, are the vehicles in the portfolio, which is made up of all of your financial products. I use different tools for each person, depending on the person, their situation and their needs. I might suggest mutual funds (which are essentially a basket of different stocks), Guaranteed Investment Certificates (GIC), or cash; and bonds, either government, corporate, or private bonds. Those are the different tools that we're going to use and the vehicle that we're going to put them in. Think of it like this: you've got an RRSP, and in that RRSP you might have a GIC, a mutual fund, and perhaps a little bit of cash. That's how a typical portfolio can look.

People are generally most familiar with GICs likely because we see these advertised all the time. Do I think everyone should have one? Definitely not. Every financial situation is unique. I am not going to tell everyone to get a GIC, an RDSP or an RRSP, because in some cases you have to qualify for these. Keep in mind, all of this is done inside your financial plan, so it always has to make sense for your portfolio. A GIC, however, is a very conservative, low-risk investment that usually offers a required rate of return. For example, if you hear the annual five-year GIC is 3.03%, then you will know that is the rate of return on that GIC for a fixed term of five years. This means you have to keep it in there for five years to get your 3.03%, but it is guaranteed. If the market goes up or down, it doesn't matter, because you know that is exactly what you will get. This is what makes it conservative.

Guaranteed Investment Certificates are predictable, which can lead people to believe they are safe. Personally, I don't like to use the word "safe" in reference to GICs because it's important to be discerning when it comes to considering something safe. If your money isn't growing, that's not necessarily very safe. This is something you might ask your advisor about as you establish what you are willing to accept as risk and determine your risk profile. You can always have a GIC inside your different investing vehicles, like your RRSP, something that many people do.

Let's take a closer look at some of the other potential streams of investment. In Canada, the Registered Retirement Savings Plan (RRSP) is a tool that people use to reduce their taxable income so that they're able to save more on their initial, yearly tax return. If you connect this with what I said above, where the R is "rules," in the case of the RRSP, the rules are that you have to invest money, which will reduce your taxes by a certain amount of dollars, and you will have that money invested for a tax deferred investment time. By this I mean the RRSP is part of your retirement plan so that the taxes defer until you take the money out in the future and then you pay tax at that time. It's not tax-free, it's not tax-never, it's tax deferred. You're paying tax, just not paying it today. The RRSP is then actually able to grow and compound before tax dollars are taken. As with all tools, there's a good place and time for these. RRSPs are probably the most popular retirement tool in Canada. What people forget, however, are the tax implications when they make a withdrawal, because withdrawals are 100% taxable. This simply means that you if you withdraw money from your RRSP, you pay the tax and not only that, you also are unable to reinvest that amount of money in that RRSP when you have funds available again.

A good planner might help by assessing ways to minimize the tax every time you want to make a withdrawal. You always want to keep more in your pocket than in someone else's. To minimize tax you could have different vehicles for retirement so you're not just feeding your RRSPs. When you withdraw your money, you don't take it all out of an RRSP; you take it from different areas as well. This way, 100% of your money isn't all 100% taxable.

The RRSP amount is going to reduce your taxable income on your tax return. Many people ask me how much they have for an RRSP contribution limit, but they have no idea how it's calculated. As of writing this book, the contribution limit is 18% of your previous year's earned income up to $26,010. This is the most that you can contribute to an RRSP. An unused contribution can be carried forward indefinitely, so it can be carried forward to the next year. Contributions are deductible for the previous year if you've made them within 60 days of year-end. That's why people call the first two months of the new year "RRSP season." I'm not, personally, a fan of this "RRSP season". I believe good planning all year eliminates the need of this mad rush of investing in that short period of time.

As I said, contributions can be can carried forward indefinitely and deducted in a future year. If you invest today, and you don't actually need the deduction, you can carry it forward to next year and use it against your taxes at that time. Contributions to an individual RRSP may be made up to and including the year in which you turn 71. By December 31st of that year, your RRSP must be de-registered or transferred to our next acronym, RRIF, or Registered Retirement Income Fund.

A RRIF is the successor to the RRSP. With a RRIF, your money gets invested and it stays invested until it starts to be withdrawn. This is the point where you are required to start making withdrawals.

What if you don't withdraw anything? You're retired; you're now at the age of 71. You have to convert all your RRSPs into the RRIF. Then you have to start taking the minimum amount of your RRIF out. You're required by age 71 to start paying some tax. This can be the minimum amount, depending on your income. The RRSP has grown on a tax-deferred basis, and now it is converted to the RRIF and you have to make the minimum annual withdrawal which means you now must start paying tax. Payments received from a RRIF are included in your income the year they're withdrawn. When you take your money out of your RRIF, as you have to, you're going to pay tax on it. It's 100% taxable because it's now counted as your income. You can't use that as a write-off again. By the time you're 91, all the tax has to be paid on the amount you put into the RRIF, whether you need the money or not.

In some cases, people know how much they want to withdraw every year, and this can be set up as an automatic withdrawal. Either way, investors (i.e. you) should re-balance their portfolio when they retire to make sure they have enough income for the short- and long-term and to make sure the risk of their investment matches their risk tolerance as they get older. Usually risk tolerance decreases with age.

The next vehicle I mentioned above is a Registered Disability Savings Plan, or RDSP. This is a plan that a lot of

116

people qualify for and don't even know it. This plan is for my Canadian friends only. To qualify, you have to be a resident of Canada, under the age of 59, with a valid social insurance number, and be a recipient of the Disability Tax Credit. It's helpful to work with someone like me when it comes to getting the paperwork and application complete. While you can apply on your own, you need an advisor who's licensed to be able to work with the investment aspect of this plan. You are also not required to deposit any money into an investment; but obviously if the Government is going to give you approximately $3 for every $1 that you invest, you might want to consider it. Of course, this is based on the rules and requirements set out under the RDSP guidelines. They, like other government registered plans, may change each year, so it's important to work with someone who knows the rules.

The RDSP works similarly to the RRSP. The money that you contribute grows for your retirement and you don't pay tax on it right away. There are some restrictions on withdrawals so you can't just go and take money out at any time. It's helpful, because if you have a disability, this forces you to save your money. There are two other aspects to this: the Canada Disability Savings Grant (CDSG) and the Canada Disability Savings Bond (CDSB). The CDSG is a matching grant from the government that is deposited directly into your RDSP. Through these grants the government matches 300, 200, or 100%, depending on the amount you contribute, to a maximum of $3500 a year, with a lifetime maximum of $70,000. This is also based on your family's net income. With the CDSB, the government deposits money into your RDSP. If you qualify, you could receive up to $1,000 a year with a lifetime of $20,000. This is a really useful investment for people who have the DTC and qualify for the RDSP.

Then we come to the Tax-Free Savings Account, or TFSA. Most people think of this as a bank account, but you can also invest inside of a TFSA. In fact, the TFSA was set up by the government with the initial intention of helping people get started investing. In my opinion the TFSA is one of the best tools for investing, with the worst name because people think it should be set up as a bank account. The TFSA has a maximum contribution limit but the amount of your allowance is based on your age. There are investment funds that you can use for the TFSA that can offer really good rates of returns. It's also 100% tax free. The growth is tax free; when you make a withdrawal.. With a TFSA, you don't lose your allowance for contributions, as opposed to with the RRSP. The allowance is capped every year, however, so there is still a limit on what you can contribute.

The TFSA is one of the best investment tools available, because you can invest almost any of the funds that you would invest in an RRSP in the TFSA. It's a great tool, because it's tax free. It is not tax deferred, not tax later, not tax ever, tax free. When you invest your money in this particular vehicle and grow your money, all of that growth is tax free. Apart from the fact that you have to be Canadian and over 18, anyone reading this can set up a TFSA today. If you're 18 years old today, you can start a TFSA, and you will have a $5,500 maximum contribution allowance. This maximum allowance may change each year, and it has in the past due to changes in government. Unlike the RRSP, if you were to withdraw contributions, you're allowed to put them back in. If you take out $1,000, you can put $1,000 back in. Of course, you'll want to talk with your advisor and make sure you do it right in terms of timing, but you don't lose the contribution allowance room; and the withdrawals are not only tax free, you can use them for anything you want. There are no restrictions. Any amount can be withdrawn at any time and it can be re-contributed in the future if you want to. A TFSA may be close in description to a Roth IRA in the U.S.

Another major investment most families make in a lifetime is in their children, most obviously through their university or college tuition. The Registered Education Savings Plan (RESP) is an investment tool for people who have children and want to invest in their education. With this plan, you invest your money and it is tax deferred, and you also may qualify for a government grant contribution towards your children's education. It's helpful to get these set up as early as possible in your child's life.

Your advisor will have to apply for the government contribution when they set up your RESP, and it's always a good practice for you to periodically check and see that it's making money and the contribution is coming in. If your advisor forgets to apply for the government grant, you can lose out on the 20% contribution, for example. A RESP goes towards any education, whether university, college, trade school, or continuing education.

While you can set up these plans yourself, I highly recommend working with an advisor. Working with an advisor should help you get the best returns, since their job is to review the different funds available, something most people either don't make the time to do, have no idea where to start looking, or don't have access to.

If you work with an advisor, it's best to make the whole investment plan with the same person. Don't have your RRSP with one advisor and your TFSA with another. It makes it easier to see the whole plan and review it all together at the same time every year. It also helps when adjustments need to be made to the plan, as this way the advisor will know where everything is and what the goal is for you overall. Most importantly working with one advisor better ensures no errors in over-contribution to RRSP, TFSA, RESP, or other plans.

All of these plans can be used to help yourself become more tax efficient. First, you have to figure out what you think you'll need and when you plan to retire. The RRSP is part of your plan when it comes to planning for your taxes. It's not going to be all RRSP or TFSA; it all depends on your particular plan. Your advisor will help you do a risk analysis to see what your level of risk is, and from there they recommend the funds that will perform best for your profile.

This goes for RRSP, TFSA, and RESPs but you still have to do it on an individual basis. For instance, an RESP is only for people with kids, so that's not going to be part of your plan if you don't have any kids. If you're planning on having kids you might keep it in the back of your mind. You're the one who knows whether you will have kids or not, and the advisor is there to work with you whatever your decision is. If I'm sitting with a couple and they say, "You know what? We're planning on having kids in a year," then I'd be thinking about whether we're going to set up an RESP for these kids and, if so, how much my clients will need to get it started. This way we'd plan to have a dollar amount ready to set up an RESP once the baby is born.

It might feel overwhelming at first, all these acronyms and understanding what you have and where. This is why it's helpful to read your Investment Statement, a statement you always receive when you invest with an advisor. A lot of women have come to me not knowing how to read their statements; and it is tricky, given that each company may use a different layout for their statements, which means not all investment statements look exactly the same. Still, most contain general terms, and once you understand these terms, you'll find your statements more accessible to read. They still have the same information, just presented differently.

Let's look at the basics of understanding your statement. At the top there is usually a logo or an investment company name. That's the name of the fund company. Your name and contact information are below on the opposite side of your financial advisor's name and information. You'll also see it say, "Statement of Account" and the time period for statement reporting.

When you start reading down you'll see investor information, and the type of account. That's where it will say what you're invested in. In this example, it's a Registered Retirement Savings Plan, which is in Canada. That's the type of account. It could read "Open Money." It could read "Tax Free Savings Account" or something else. You will see your account number beside this. Under "Account Value" it will show your closing market value this period. That's the total amount of money you have at the end of the period. The opening balance is the total amount that you had at the beginning of the period. The book cost is the total of the original investment, which is how much you originally put into the investment.

Somewhere about halfway down, you'll see a summary of the funds in which you have invested. Under account summary, you see the funds; in this example there are two different funds in your statement of account, otherwise known as your portfolio. The document tells you what the

# INVESTMENT COMPANY

# STATEMENT OF ACCOUNT
July 01, 2017 to September 30, 2017

**JANE DOE**
123 HOME ST
ANYWHERE, ON A1B 2C3

*Your Financial Advisor*
MARY SMITH
ADVISOR COMPANY
789 WORK ST. UNIT 1
SOMEWHERE ON 29X8W7

## Investor Information

| *Account Type* | *Account Number* |
|---|---|
| **Registered Retirement Savings Plan** | *12345* |

These investments are registered in your name at

## Account Value

| | |
|---|---|
| Closing Market Value This Period | $ 112,771.27 |
| Opening Balance | $ 123,984.55 |
| Book Cost | $ 112,387.91 |

## Account Summary

| Fund Name | DSC | Book Cost ($) | Average Cost ($) | Unit Balance | Unit Price ($) | Market Value ($) |
|---|---|---|---|---|---|---|
| Canadian $ Investments | | | | | | |
| **FUND GLOBAL A CODE 567** | N | 3,66.49 | 13,3876 | 274.096 | 13,11011 | 3,607.40 |
| **FUND GLOBAL A CODE 246** | Y | 108,718.42 | 13,1074 | 8,294.431 | 13.1611 | 109,163.84 |
| TOTAL Canadian $ Investments | | 112,387.91 | | | | 112,771.24 |

"**Book Cost**" means the total amount paid to purchase an investment, including any transaction charges related to the purchase, adjusted for reinvested distributions, return of capital and corporate reorganizations.
The book (original) cost shown in this statement may not be suitable for income tax purposes, as it may not reflect all required adjustments. It is important for you to keep records of all of your investment transactions and consult your income tax advisor to properly determine your gains and losses for income tax purposes.

"**Market value**" is the price at which an investment can be sold on the open market at a specific point in time. The market value of an investment fund is its "**Net Asset Value**". This is usually calculated by investment managers once per day/week/month.

If you chose a deferred sales charge (DSC) option when you purchased units of a mutual fund, a sales charge may be payable by you when you sell your units. The sales charge is deducted form the amount you receive for your units. It is usually based on what you paid when you purchase your units. This sales charge usually declines to zero after you have owned the units for a specific number of years.
There are some variations in how DSCs are calculated. For specific information about the DSC for the units that you own, check the Fund Facts documents for each of your funds or contact your financial advisor.

### Percentage of Holdings

▇▇ 3.2% FUND GLOBAL A CODE 567      ☐ 96.80% FUND GLOBAL A CODE 246

## Contributions Summary

| | |
|---|---|
| RSP First 60 Days | $0.00 |
| RSP Remainder of Year | $0.00 |

## Transaction Summary

| Fund Name | Purchases & Transfer-In ($) | Redemptions & Transfers-Out ($) | Income Distribution ($) | Capital Gain Distribution ($) |
|---|---|---|---|---|
| FUND GLOBAL A CODE 567 | | | | |
| FUND GLOBAL A CODE 246 | | | | |

Any switch activity within your account is reported in the transaction details section of your statement.

## Transaction Details

| Trade Date | Transaction Type | Gross Amount ($) | Deductions Amount ($) | Net Amount ($) | Unit Price ($) | Transaction Units | Unit Balance |
|---|---|---|---|---|---|---|---|
| **FUND GLOBAL A CODE 567** | | | | | | | |
| Opening Balance | | | | | | | 1,028.823 |
| 06/30/2017 | Redemption | 10,000.00 | 2,147.41 | 7,852.59 | 13,3027 | 751.727 | 274.096 |
| Closing Balance | | | | | | | 2740096 |
| **FUND GLOBAL A CODE 246** | | | | | | | |
| Opening Balance | | | | | | | 8,294.31 |
| Closing Balance | | | | | | | 8,294.31 |

Please review your statement of account carefully. If there is any information that does not match your records, contact your Financial Advisor or our Client Services department within 60 days.



Download this sample statement here:

https://womensinvestmentandsocialexchange.com/free-resources/

codes are. Here you will see that Fund A has X amount of dollars in it. You might have two funds, so you have Fund B and that has Y amount of dollars in it. The total of that is the total amount of your portfolio, so X plus Y is your portfolio. The letters "DSC" stand for deferred sales charge. This is the commission set up for the fund. The commitment may be for 5 years for example and; thus, there may be a penalty for early withdrawal. You'll see the first fund has an N which means no, there's no penalty. The second one is a Y which means yes there is a penalty, so if you withdraw money you have to pay a penalty to take the money out.

Further down, or possibly on the next page, you'll see more details for each fund. You should be able to see the book value and market value. Book cost is the same as at the top. That's your original amount of the investment. The average cost is how much per share your funds are. The unit balance is how many units that you own in that particular fund. The book value is how much you've taken and invested. For instance, if you took $10,000 and invested it, it's now worth a market value of $12,000. The growth is $2,000. You will also see the growth period, or the time it took for your investment to grow. The graph at the bottom shows you the percentage of holding. In this example, you'll see 3.2% of your total holdings are in fund A, and 96.8% are in fund B, the second fund.

Beneath the value of your investment you'll find more details. It's not unlike a bank statement recording of your withdrawals and deposits, only this one says "switch," "withdrawal" or "reinvested dividends" if you have taken money out. A "switch" is when you move money from one fund to another fund. A withdrawal is just like in banking when you physically take money out. To reinvest your dividends is simply to reinvest the dividend-paying stocks in the funds you've invested in back into your account. Reinvested dividends are part of the beauty of the compounding. The money just automatically gets put back in.

When you look at the second page you'll see the contribution summary. If you contributed RSPs in the first 60 days, this shows you how much. In this case there's zero. If you contributed any of the remainder of the day, or remainder of the year, it will show that, although in this example it shows zero. When you contribute is important based on how you file your taxes and what you account for.

The transaction summary is where any new money that gets transferred or added into your account will be shown for this period; in this case, it's zero. Redemption is if any money's withdrawn or transferred out. In this example, we have $10,000 withdrawn from the first fund.

The transaction detail at the bottom reveals more information about the withdrawal. You'll see what the name of the fund is that the withdrawal came from, which in this example is code 567. Then you see the gross amount, which is S10,000, the date that it was redeemed or withdrawn, and the deduction amount, in this case, $2,147.41. That's the taxes withheld or the penalties or fee that apply to it. The net amount is the total that you receive in your account. The unit price is how much each unit was redeemed at; in this case, the number of units that was cashed in is 751.727.

The unit balance shows you how many shares are left in that fund. At the start of the period you had 1,025.823 and at the end, after you deduct your 751.727, you have 274.096 shares or units of shares in that fund.

The information at the bottom (address, phone number, fax) is the contact information of your fund company. Beside this is the beginning and end balance; and in this example, since there was nothing redeemed or added to this fund, the beginning balance and ending balance of units is the same.

If you enjoy investing solo and are not working with a financial advisor, you're always able to get a second opinion. Some advisors may charge you a fee, but if you're feeling doubtful, it's always worth it to have that second opinion. Looking at your investment statement regularly keeps you aware of the movement of your investments. Most people want to know, after they've invested $10,000, do they have $12,000 now? Or $6,000? Are you making money or not making money? If you invested $10,000 ten years ago and it's only worth $11,000 today, that may not be considered a great return to you and it's going to take a long time to reach your goal of financial freedom. In a case like that, you definitely want to get another opinion and advice.

▼ **If you have questions about your statement, there are a few things you can do:**

1. Go ask your financial advisor to help you read and understand your statement.

2. If you don't have a financial advisor, ask someone you trust (family member or money-savvy friend).

3. Join the W.I.S.E Women community at **www.womenwise.ca** where I go into more detail on how to read your specific statement.

4. Get a second opinion. Ask another financial advisor to double-check your statement.

However you decide to do it, don't be daunted by investing! You also don't need to have thousands of dollars already saved up to start. Start right now. Even $10 a month in a TFSA can start compounding and adding up over time. There are many financial advisors ready and waiting to help you navigate the world of investments. Investments have made many wealthy people much wealthier, and it's not exclusive to the rich. We all have access to investing on some level, so take advantage of what's available and begin your long-term savings.

# Chapter 10

# Retire with Ease

*"If you think investing is risky, wait until you get the bill for not investing,"*

*"Your personal philosophy is your greatest determining factor in how your life works out."*

-JIM ROHN

There is more to retirement than just money. Planning for retirement involves psychological as well as financial preparation. What will you do with your time? Will you volunteer for a charity? Which charity? Will you play golf? Cards? Join a group? Then there are the questions of will I have enough to retire on? How long will my money last? Will I outlast my money or will it outlast me? We know we need money to live and as such, it makes sense that we need to plan to have money around for as long as we plan to be around ourselves. Retirement planning is a natural part of anyone's financial life. Most people work at jobs that help with retirement or provide a pension, but many of us don't and the trend is that fewer companies are adding or expanding pensions. In fact, many pensions have been eliminated or reduced. Regardless of whether you're in a career that will end at 65 and contribute to your pension or not, considering how you want your elder years to look and how you want to care for yourself financially during that time is a must. You also want to look at long-term health care needs, travel insurance needs, and your legacy desires.

It's never too late to take care of yourself as you get older. Sure, you may not have a lot of time to let compounding really work, and sometimes it's too late to get certain life insurance products, but rest assured, you can always do something.

Some investment products can be pricey for people beyond age 65, such as life insurance policies. However, investments can still be set up and contributed to. Even if you're 60 years old you can start saving and investing for your remaining work years. It may not be the optimum plan but you can certainly do a plan that works for you. You can still do some tax planning and estate planning at any age.

The best advice is not to wait. Of course, it's optimal to start your retirement planning when you're 20, although I rarely meet a 20-year-old who's interested in planning for retirement! Although the ones I do meet were disciplined in savings from an early age and know how to have their money work for them. They also get very excited when they see how their money can grow over the next 40 or 50 years. I work with a lot of women in their middle years, 30s and 40s, and I get them on track for retirement saving right away. Starting at 40, at least, gives you a good 25 years. Remember, just because you turn 65 and retire, you're not withdrawing every cent you own; you take what you need, which leaves the rest to continue compounding for potentially another 20 years or more.

The investments still stay invested, which means they are still working for you and making your money grow. With help from your advisor, you may make changes or adjustments as to what the investment fund is because your risk tolerance might change, or you now require an income stream. All this is part of the ongoing annual reviews with your advisor. The preparation is done in advance, the planning is in place and the plan gets executed. This is why it is important to build a relationship with your advisor and work with that person you trust so you can implement the plans you have for yourself and your family. Having your goals mapped out and knowing what direction you want to head in are keys to success.

Sometimes women ask me if they can retire based on their investments. They might be closer to 35 in age, and they'll want to know if they can make and have $1 million when they retire. To figure this out, we reverse engineer to determine how much they need to invest to produce $1 million, give or take, and depending on market conditions. This means, we start with the goal in mind. In this example, we start with $1 million, then calculate how much needs to be invested over the next 30 years, assuming retirement age is 65, and what average expected rate of return we can reasonably look to on the investments.

Most people have a number in mind when it comes to what they want to retire with. People hear $1 million and think that's a lot of money, but everybody handles $1 million differently over the course of their life. I find that when you start to talk about $1 million to people, it seems unattainable or even fantasy to them. However, when I ask how much do you need each year when you're retired, it's easier to understand $80,000 or $65,000 per year or any other number that is something they can comprehend. It's also more realistic; that $1 million that sounds so dreamy is only going to give you 12 years of an $80,000 a year lifestyle. That's potentially going to last you until you're 77; what if you live to be 95?

Furthermore, having $1 million that is 100% taxable is a whole different story than $1 million with little tax. Remember the TFSA? If you were investing with your TFSA and maxed out the contribution allowance every year, when you retire, if the account is worth $1 million then all of it would be yours to use as you see fit, no taxes to pay. You may really need a few million dollars in order to have $1 million before tax. That's got to be the number that carries you through however many years you have left. Taxes always take a big chunk out of your retirement fund, so it's important to be tax efficient.

Working with an advisor helps you improve in this area. We know what different baskets we can pull from so you don't have to pay tax on everything. The reality is, most Canadians use their RRSP as their only, or at least their main, retirement vehicle, or they rely on a pension, if they have one, as their main retirement vehicle. Both of these are fully taxable.

Retirement is a funny topic for people. If they don't plan for it, they don't seem to get there. Further, I've seen a lot of people fear retirement. They feel like it's the end for them and there's nothing else. I think this is because we all know retirement isn't just about money. Retirement is about planning for your time as well as your money. Your money has to outlive you or at least live long enough to get you through your retirement, but you also have to have a plan. You can't just be doing work today and have nothing to do tomorrow. You have to line up something to do, whether it's part time work or volunteer work with different educational or charity organizations. If you want to retire and travel the world, the amount of money you need to plan for versus retire and babysit your grandkids is very different.

Write a book, start exercising, take up a hobby. There has to be planning on the retirement side that is not just about finances. Having said that, it helps to establish precisely when you want to retire in the first place. Once I know this, I back-engineer it with my clients. If my client says she wants to retire at 65, I look at what she has now and what she needs to save so that she has enough money to last her through the retirement.

In Canada, both the Canada Pension Plan (CPP) and Old Age Security (OAS) become available at retirement. Retirement in this case is 65 years old. There are provisions for the CPP to be received as early as age 60, but there is a significant claw back of the amount you are allowed to receive. The maximum amount that can be received for those starting CPP at age 65 in 2018, is $1134.17 per month. For OAS, this is $586.66 per month, according to the government website. That's $1720.83 per month, maximum. Not everyone qualifies for the maximum as it is based on how long you have made contribution amounts and how much you have been making in contributions. This is not the total you should rely on for retirement, however. When you retire you still have groceries to buy, property taxes to pay (if in a house), rent to pay (if in an apartment), condominium fees to pay (if in a condominium), car insurance, utilities, toothpaste, and all the rest. The amount the government gives you, I believe, is not enough to sustain your lifestyle plus add travel or hobbies or charitable giving to your budget, to name a few desirable expenses.

Retirement can last for twenty or thirty years, so we have to have enough money to see us through. People need to decide if they're going to be travelling in their retirement and, if so, do they have insurance to cover them? As a senior traveller, chances are you're a higher risk to get any kind of life or disability or even travel insurance. You can get travel insurance as part of a dis-ability package. These take up to age 70 or 75, so that's always in place. You just have to consider what your plans are and what it will look like when you get there. This is why I help people with the full plan, not just the financial plan. You have to be ready with the time and you have to be ready with your mindset.

Retirement planning and estate planning go together. When you are calculating what amount of money you need for your retirement, you are also looking at how that money gets handled when you're not here. That is estate planning. You need to consider all the pieces discussed in the estate section as well as final expenses. Final expenses can be paid for through a life insurance policy. There is actually final expense insurance, if you don't have life insurance already. However, if you have a lot of investments then you need to look at whether or not you need to earmark certain money for your final expenses as part of your plan. Of course, your final wishes will be clearly documented in your will. You also want to make sure you keep your will current. It's nat-ural to update your will when you retire because you have downsized your house, you may have sold that second vehi-cle, whatever the case may be.

The closer you get to tracking your spending, knowing your numbers, and amassing solid investments with an advisor, the easier you'll find planning for retirement. Once you really sit down and calculate how much you want per year, then you can work towards that goal. Chances of you meeting a concrete financial goal are higher than trying to meet some number that you pulled out of your dreams (like the ubiquitous $1 million). Take the time you need to both prepare your psychological plan and your financial plan for retirement. It's the least you can do for yourself after a long life spent working hard and earning.

Retirement can be a beautiful time of life for people, and you can make it beautiful for yourself, too, by devoting a little time right now to preparing for it.

# Chapter 11

# Teaching Kids About Money

*"Having high expectations is the key to everything."*

-SAM WALTON

One question I wish more people would ask is, "How do I set my kids up for the future?" It's so easy to set your kids up to have a great future. If every generation did that, can you imagine what that would do to the economy? If every parent set their kid up for financial success financially we would have a very healthy society of people who are financially responsible, pay attention to their money, and don't rely on the government to take care of their retirement or if they get hurt or ill. It's possible to have a generation of self-sufficient adults. It doesn't take a lot to make a big difference. As we saw earlier, a $10 per month investment can grow to a decent amount of money, almost $45,000, albeit that is not the only investment that is required for a sustainable retirement.

Teaching our children financial responsibility translates into less stress on social services. It can also have a profound impact on philanthropy. I believe if people are not under financial stress then they are more likely to be generous with charity, help those that are in need and be more responsible with other resources.

On the other side of this coin (no pun intended), I have talked to many parents who believe they should *not* set their children up financially, because they didn't have that same benefit. They want their kids to work for their retirement and savings. I understand that philosophy, too.

It's really a balancing act between wanting to help your children and doing it for them. You want to make them responsible, caring adults that will be a positive influence on the society they live in. I have seen wealthy parents who give their children everything with no expectation of work ethic or responsibility so I understand the fear that some parents have of providing too much for their children. Instead, I would suggest that you assist them in understanding how money works, the importance or tracking your cash, the way something like $10 per month can grow into almost $45,000. You can help them understand what protecting your income means, and what critical illness insurance is and whether or not they would need it.

I'm blessed with four beautiful step-children and I am always grateful that we get along and always have. We support each other and offer advice when needed. I have really learned what a healthy family interaction looks like. My husband and I gifted our children life insurance on Christmas. We didn't include it as part of the Christmas hoopla, we just sat together in the living room. We handed each of our kids two pieces of paper, one which told them what they're insured for and the monthly payment, and one which showed the potential growth for the investment. It was really conservative, but they'll have it for a long time.

The kids received it with varying levels of interest. I thought my daughter wasn't paying attention, yet when we went through it all together she was the one studying it the most seriously. She asked her father and me, "Why don't all parents do this for the kids?" I thought, "Holy cow! She's right," and she was the one I thought wasn't paying attention.

There are a lot of families who believe they can't afford to do anything, and that might be the case at that particular moment. However, even if they set up a plan without actually putting it into action, and share that with their kids, it will start them on a path of learning. Even if we hadn't actually established the universal life insurance policy for the kids, we would have shown them the illustration so they could see what is possible. They also are old enough that they might want to do it themselves. If the parents can't afford to make the plan themselves, it's just as valuable to share the knowledge with the kids so they can start to formulate their own plans. Introduce them to your own advisor or encourage them to talk to one they are more comfortable with. Help them to set up a plan for themselves. It's never too early to start planning for the future.

I feel grateful because I have the information and education to set my kids up like this. I can't guarantee they won't become reckless spenders, or have things happen to them like health challenges, but I know that I've done my best for my kids and their future security.

I'd encourage anyone interested in educating their kids to begin by just discussing money with them. Parents talk to their kids about drugs. They talk to their kids about drinking and grades. They talk to their kids about driving and when they get to use the car. Money should just be one of those things. Instead, money is one of those forbidden topics in general for people to talk about. Many parents won't even bring up the topic to their kids. You don't have to sit down and disclose your finances with your kids, but there's nothing wrong with teaching them bits and pieces as they go along.

Giving your child an allowance is a good introduction to learning to manage their money. Let me clarify: I believe allowances are fine, but I disagree with kids receiving an allowance because they're doing a particular chore in the house. Chores are their contribution to the house. Just because you're 13 years old doesn't mean you shouldn't have some responsibility. Anyone in the family can take out the garbage, or sweep the floor: that's their contribution as a member of the household.

An allowance is for doing something outside of your regular chores; activities like sweeping up the yard, getting the groceries, making dinner, or something to that effect. There's nothing wrong with giving an allowance for performance, either. Maybe they get their homework done on time. Being in school is your job as a kid, so you have to go, but the allowance can be tied to doing a better job at school, or exceeding expectations.

Never just give your kids money for the sake of giving money because that's not how it works in the real world. There has to be information tied to it. You don't just get this because you woke up this morning. Whenever you do give your kids money, talk to them about it.

I also think it's worth talking about investing with your kids. Kids understand what Disney is. They understand what Nike is. Teenagers and college-aged kids understand Starbucks. Now tell them they can buy stocks in those companies, and those stocks are part of what's called a mutual fund, and see what they think. Telling your kids they can invest in Starbucks changes their perception and starts to give them the understanding that money is a tool, and that how they use it can be quite empowering. They also come to realize that if they spend two dollars at Starbucks today, that can't be used for their future; whereas if they put that same two dollars into an investment, it will be worth more in the future because it will compound. Owning a mutual fund is like owning a collection of stocks in various companies. That means, if you own stocks in Starbucks, you actually own a piece of Starbucks and that's a pretty cool feeling.

You can teach them to make wiser decisions about what they want to spend their money on, so they're not just out there buying the latest fad or updating their phone every time the newest one comes out. They'll start to think that if they save a little bit, they'll have more money; and that if they start younger, they can retire earlier if they want to. You're giving them options and teaching them to make choices based on what they want to do, not what they have to do because the money's dictating it.

When they start working, this is the time to guide them as they learn how to handle their money. For instance, say your 15-year-old daughter gets a part-time job at a coffee shop. She makes $200 weekly. You might offer to her a deal like this: every time she brings home $200, she gives you half and you'll invest it. Only you won't just invest it – you'll show her how and get her involved. You can show her how her money will grow, then let her blow the other half on whatever she wants. She'll start to feel responsible, and as soon as she sees her money growing, she'll be happy to keep giving half. She's forming the habit of saving money and not spending her whole paycheque. With that mindset, you're raising a girl who will know how to save and invest, so when she finishes school, college or university or whatever, and starts her first full-time job, she'll be wise with how she uses her paycheques.

By involving your daughter right from the start, her financial education becomes experiential. You're not lecturing her or telling her what to do; she's doing it alongside you and you're both engaged in the process. A lot of parents don't do this because they don't even know about finances themselves. If money has never been discussed in the household, it's hard to know where to begin.

All families, in all income brackets, can start a conversation about money. They can learn together, focus on what they really want as a family and as individuals and help each other focus on their goals. When you involve the kids in the process, they start to see that it doesn't have to be a sacrifice; you are removing the negative connotation that gets attached to money, that belief that we always have to sacrifice something now in order to have something else in the future. When you present it in a fun way, the kids will see that they get to have fun, go to the movies, buy that video game, yet still have a secure future because they put hard work into it.

The children are thus rewarded on both ends, and so are you. Instead of hearing kids bemoaning how they can't do what they want because they "have to save for the future," they still have fun and live in the now and enjoy their lives. It also teaches them to prioritize what they really want to spend their money on. It helps them appreciate what they have and they will be more responsible because they know what it takes to replace something if they are careless. They will understand the importance of hard work and being aware of the opportunities that exist about where they can put their money: either spend it or save it.

Eventually, it's student-loan time. If an RESP isn't set up, it's likely the child will have to get a loan, so then someone like me might have to work with them to make a plan to pay off their debt. There's not a lot you can do about it at that point, except work it into the plan. Knowing the interest rate, how it will be paid, if you can expedite the payoff and what rules exist surrounding the loan all come into the plan, too.

If the loan is an Ontario government student loan, like the Ontario Student Assistance Program (OSAP) for example, the rules on when you pay it back with the interest rate are different than if you just took out a student line of credit. Also, if you apply for OSAP or bank loans, you still have to qualify based on the criteria they have. Right now, the OSAP is set up for students to begin paying it back after they've graduated. That means they finish their academic career in debt, with no guarantee of employment.

A student line of credit at the bank works similarly to a home equity line of credit; it's just a line of credit that goes up and down. As long as they're paying the interest on it they can adjust how much they're paying each month. If one month they put $500 down on it and the next month they only put $400 on it they're still okay. They're not going to get in trouble. It depends on what stage they're at.

If you didn't set up an RESP when your kids were young, you could still set one up if they're 15 or younger; older than that gets into special rules. Setting one up later in your child's life just means you have less time for the money to grow, so it doesn't make the most sense. At 18, approximately, is when they start withdrawing on it.

Whether they have a RESP or have to apply for a loan in order to go to school, it's important to understand how the money works. For instance, with a RESP, you have to start early, contribute to the investment, apply for government grants, if applicable, and figure out if the investment will generate enough for the total education plan. Depending on when the RESP gets started, how much is contributed, how long new money is added, whether or not government grants apply, it will affect how much is available for school. Sometimes it still isn't enough.

Not all parents are prepared to pay for their kid's education. If that's the case, you have to approach it differently because the parents' income may still be a deciding factor in what the child can qualify for. Even if the family has low income I would still advise them to open the RESP. This is where an advisor becomes very helpful because there are ways to open the RESP with no money from the parents but still get money deposited, even if it is a small amount. At least it is some money for the family/child that will have the same compounding growth advantages.

Talking to your kids about money is important in so many ways, not just for their education.

They always say there are two guarantees: taxes and death. We know what's going to happen; we just don't know when. When your kids get older and they're young adults, you want them to be comfortable with what happens when you're no longer around. You don't want the kids to be surprised. They're going to be sad, and they're going to be in mourning, so you don't want that transition to be overwhelmingly difficult for them because they now also have to deal with the estate.

There's nothing wrong with having a conversation to let your kids know what you've decided, who is the executor, how it all works and where the information lives. Remind them they don't have to worry about it until the day comes. It's about eliminating stress and being overwhelmed when the day comes. This conversation will leave the kids with more understanding of what to expect. It also serves to get them thinking about how they'll be buying a house and investing and will need to do estate planning as they get older, themselves. By having the conversation with them early on, you're paving the way for them to start thinking about their own plans.

Sometimes your kids might not be ready to hear it, which happens. It's like any other topic. You just test the water, and when you see that they're not ready for it, that's fine: you leave it. You can keep dropping comments and this gets them accustomed to it. It also doesn't have to be a formal sit-down, in-depth conversation. It can be casual and light-hearted.

For most kids, it's just that they don't want to think about something happening to their parents. There are always opportunities to have the conversation, though; someone's mother might have become ill, or someone else's father died suddenly. These kinds of events make good opportunities to initiate conversation. What you really want to teach kids is the habit of knowing their finances and their estate and understanding it.

As parents, it's really up to us to educate our kids when it comes to money. Real-life math and economics is not commonly taught in schools and for generations it has been left to the parents to disseminate this information. Don't let money become a taboo topic in your household; by opening up the conversation and welcoming your children into it, guiding them along the way, we have the potential to create an entirely new generation of financially literate adults.

# Conclusion

-SIMON SINEK

For the first 40 years of my life, I was behind-the-scenes. If things had not happened as they did, I never would have left the family business and I wouldn't be doing what I'm doing now. I never would have taken the time for me. I used to do everything else first for everyone, just like so many women. Now I take care of myself first and empower other women to do the same.

Looking back, I don't regret any of it. I don't regret the years it took to complete three master's degrees, and I don't regret the tough life lessons learned from the family business. There is no such thing as mistakes, only lessons learned. Nothing is a waste of time. You always get something out of it. All you need is that one piece of information that leads you. That one course, that one seminar; you just never know when you will find it. We have to balance enjoying our lives and having fun with saving for our futures and being responsible. Enjoy today and plan for tomorrow. I hope this book will help you to do that.

No matter where you are in life, or how much money you have or don't have, you can always do something to set yourself on the track to financial freedom. If nothing else, make sure you've at least got a will. Make sure your wishes are clearly known. If you have kids, or pets, whatever makes up your family, make sure they are protected and will be looked after if you're no longer around. Everyone can get a will, and there are so many affordable ways to get a will done.

Look at everything you have, put it all in one spot; know where your bank accounts are. If you have investments and life insurance, make sure it's all together and someone knows where it is. You don't go through this whole life putting all these things into play only so nobody can find them. Every single person can get their estate organized and every single person can have a will stating what they want to have happen.

It's a common expression these days that you are the reflection of the five people you hang around with the most. The same is true with your finances. If you hang around with a bunch of women who are scared or frustrated with their finances, then you're going to stay scared and frustrated about your finances. But if you join a community or have a friendship with somebody who isn't afraid to talk about money, and money doesn't get treated as a taboo conversation or topic, then you'll feel calmer talking about it. The more you talk about it, the more comfortable you'll feel. You'll understand it better, and then be better prepared to take action and do something about your own situation.

If the people you hang around with only discuss what reality show they watched on TV last night, you're never going to learn about your finances. You're never going to move past that frustrated or scared stage or become comfortable understanding your statements. You will never feel comfortable asking questions and possibly feel stupid when you talk to somebody about finance, because you're not having regular conversations about it. You're not looking at it as a regular topic.

If you want to learn public speaking, you join a group like Toastmasters. Then you might take your friends there so that you can all learn better speaking techniques. You can do the same thing with your finances. Make a conscious choice to have a conversation with your friends about money. Find out what they know, who they've worked with. Be open and honest about your emotions about money. You don't have to disclose everything about your own status, unless you want to; and if you do, you can ask your friends to keep it confidential. Still, even just a general conversation about money with your friends will yield a better understanding, and doubtless reduce stress, for all of you.

This book is only the beginning of your love affair with your money, yourself and your new lifestyle. If you're eager to find like-minded women, to keep learning and continue the conversation, there is a whole lot more fun for you over at www.womenwise.ca

I started the Women's Investment and Social Exchange (W.I.S.E.) group after recognizing that so many women I knew, friends, clients, and colleagues, were scared of finance. None of them had grown up in households that discussed money. Most of them relied on their husbands. None of them wanted to appear stupid when they asked questions. They felt comfortable discussing financial concepts with a group of women who were like them. The more people knew me, the more they'd spread the news to their friends. "Ask Kathy," they'd offer, "She probably knows." I loved it. I loved finance, so people knew to ask me questions.

When I formed the group, it was to gather women to discuss and learn about money. Women are smart and capable of knowing all of this. So many women are scared because they don't know what they don't know. Further, they don't know where to go to get the information they need, and they want to be comfortable in whatever environment they are in to be able to ask questions and not feel foolish. My group began rather casually, going from gathering over wine to growing into a fantastic online community. Of course, there may still be wine involved in the face-to-face gatherings that we aim to hold. Our group is about building a community of financially empowered women while still enjoying social time together.

Ongoing support and community are critical for success in any area of your life. One of the biggest factors in our own ongoing success and wealth-building has been the posse of women holding one another accountable, being guides for each other, cheering one another on and supporting each other's goals and dreams. We want this for you, too.

We've put together resources, education, programs, tools, and ongoing support for you. Join us at www.womenwise.ca and learn how you can:

**1. Join our exclusive community.** Connect with other people reading the book and experiencing results. Ask questions. Give answers. Build wealth in community.

**2. Do the exercises.** Download PDFs of all the exercises in the book plus additional resources.

**3. Access podcasts, videos, recommendations, interviews and articles.** The material in this book is living and breathing in our own lives. As we build the community and continue to build our own wealth and yours, we will be sure to share updates with you on the site.

**4. Share your success.** Share your own story of building wealth and feeling empowered with your finances. Read other people's stories to keep you inspired.

**5. Join our members-only Facebook group** to stay connected with members, ask questions, share experiences and support each other on our journey to financial success.

Visit www.womenwise.ca to join in the fun and go deeper with the book. You are also welcome to visit my podcasts and live radio show at **www.inspiredchoicesnetwork.com**. Through these programs I share different tools and conversation around how money affects our lives. It's about the energy of money and the effects of stress and weight as it relates to money, as well as fun saving and planning tips. The radio show is "Financially Speaking" and available on several podcast platforms, including YouTube and iTunes. Visit the website for more information or to tune in.

Your financial future is up to you, and you have the capacity to be a wise steward of your money. It's time to stop being overwhelmed, daunted, and with your head in the sand. Read and re-read this book. Find me online, listen to my radio show, and become a WISE woman. When you set yourself up financially, you'll find your life is so much more easy, joyful, and fun. Most of all, when you are set up financially, you are empowered. You have more choices available. You can move through life proactively, not reactively. Isn't that a life worth saving for?

# Client Relationship Goals Sample

When clients first reach out to me, I sit down and we have a conversation. Please take the time to assess where you are currently with your finances and where you want to go.

**CURRENT STATUS:**

1. Describe your current financial situation:

2. Where do you want to be:

3. Describe your feelings about your current financial situation:

Ex: Overwhelmed

Frustrated

**RISK PROFILE: Novice, Fair, Good, Sophisticated**

Women almost always consider themselves as novices when it comes to assessing their skill level with respect to their finances. Women are always harder on themselves, and sell themselves short when it comes to assessing their knowledge and understanding.

Every single one of my clients undervalues their knowledge and their handle on their finances. They usually understand what I'm talking about, but they almost always label themselves as Novice or Fair, when most of them would fall in the 'Good' category.

**4. If there is one thing you could have fixed immediately, what would it be:**

Answers include:

- Kid's education

- Have debts paid off

- Have car, student loans paid off

- Make sure I have enough money for retirement so I have the same or better lifestyle than I have currently

- Travel (all-inclusive once a year, go shopping to buy what I want when I want it, Christmas shopping for grandkids, buy a pair of shoes when I want to, etc.)

**YOUR GOALS AND OBJECTIVES:**

**What are your overall personal goals/objectives/ interests:**

Examples may include:

1. To establish and maintain a monthly budget.
2. To alleviate the monthly financial burden of debt, interest, and loans while meeting financial obligations.
3. Move into a bigger house.
4. Buying own house (or being able to afford it on sole income).

**What are your primary goals/objectives for your family and what are you doing to accomplish them?**

Examples may include:

154

Primary goal is to pay off debt (i.e. credit cards, loans, mortgage and truck).

Start saving money for my children's education and establish some savings for the future.

**Short Term Goals: (1- 18 months)**

Short term goals include:

1. Review traditional vs HELOC mortgage and renew mortgage.
2. Within the next two months pay off credit cards and loans.
3. Start contributing to an RESP for the kids.
4. Start contributing to TFSA.
5. Get term insurance policy to cover mortgage instead of mortgage insurance.
6. Review bank accounts to alleviate bank fees.
7. Start savings plan for emergency fund/travel fund.
8. Start investing plan for retirement and future.
9. Review last 10 years of income tax returns, apply for Child Tax Benefit retroactively.

**Mid Term Goals: (2 – 5 years)**

Midterm goals include:

1. Build up savings and investments.
2. Build up children's education plan.
3. Pay off vehicle.

**Long Term Goals: (5 plus years)**

Long term goals include:

1. Pay off mortgage.

**What are the three things that are getting in the way of achieving your goals?**

1. Debt from marriage/separation.
2. Single income in household.
3. Require assistance with a financial plan to get on track.

**What impact will these issues have on achieving your goals?**

They will directly impact my ability to meet my financial obligations for myself and my kids and to plan for our future.

**If you don't do anything, what is likely to happen?**

If nothing gets done then there will be severe financial risk for the family to pay our monthly bills, savings and investment will not get done; thus, jeopardizing our future. If an emergency were to arise, there will be no system in place to get through it. Also, retirement may be stressful, as lifestyle may be compromised, since not planning for financial needs.

**When do you plan to retire?**

Ideally, at age 65.

**How much do you plan on needing, per year, to retire?**

It would be great to have $50,000/year to retire on.
Most people hope to have their current income, or close to it, in retirement. They want to have the same ability to do what they're doing now, plus travelling and shopping. Depending where they are at, they have to factor in inflation. $50,000/year today is going to require more money in the future, due to inflation.

**Your expectations of your advisor:**
How do you see your advisor helping you to meet your personal goals going forward?
Give some thought to what you want your advisor to do for you.

**Examples include:** Maintaining a watch on the investments, recommending changes when appropriate, meeting at least once per year to review goals and make necessary adjustments, if needed.

Providing debt consolidation advice and putting plan into place and helping Mary to stay on track with her future goals.

Our recommendations and action plan to help you succeed:

Join WISE, book Kathy to speak at your events, book an appointment with an advisor, reread parts of this book or the whole thing, download the forms referenced in the book and start to organize your finances. Also, commit to yourself to take action on one thing you have learned, even if it is just getting a will. Once you start the process you'll feel better and start to move in the direction of your dreams.

# About the Author

$\mathcal{K}$athy was born and raised in St. Thomas, Ontario, Canada. Married with children, Kathy has been a lifelong participant in her community: an active businesswoman, volunteer and concerned citizen.

Kathy's background is owning and operating a successful business and understanding the principles of exceptional service. As the former owner/operator of NAPA AutoPro and Uniglass Plus/Ziebart franchises she was privileged to be a recipient of the Free Enterprise Merit Award from the St. Thomas and District Chamber of Commerce in 2013. She works with the knowledge that success comes, not from her efforts alone, but in combination with those who are a part of the team. Together, goals are accomplished, exceptional service is rendered and success is achieved.

She worked in her family businesses for more than 20 years, while also working on the Ontario Motor Vehicle Industry Council Compensation Fund in Toronto for 8 years and taught in the business faculty at Fanshawe College.

She is a licensed Financial Advisor and works every day to help people, especially women, understand their finances and invest their money for their futures. She understands the financial challenges people face on a daily basis and has always had a passion to help those who need help to get on track, get ahead and save more of their money. Her excitement about finance and empowering women is contagious when you talk to her.

www.ingramcontent.com/pod-product-compliance
Lightning Source LLC
Chambersburg PA
CBHW061518050726
47593CB00002B/630